Medical Kidnapping: A Threat to Every Family in America Today

© March, 2016 Sophia Media – All Rights Reserved.

Medical Kidnapping: A Threat to Every Family in America Today

by Brian Shilhavy, Editor

Sophia Media
401 Congress Ave.
Suite 1540
Austin, Texas 78701
U.S.A.

ISBN: 978-0-9973804-0-8

Table Of Contents

Acknowledgments 8
Chapter 1 – Medical Kidnapping: A Threat to Every Child in America Today 10
   Medical Kidnapping is Real 12
      The Godboldo Family of Detroit 12
      The Nikolayev Family of Sacramento 14
      The Rider Family of Kansas City 18
      Justina Pelletier and Boston Children's Hospital 19
      Family of Amish Girl Who Fled the Country to Avoid Forced Experimental Chemo Tells Their Side of the Story 21
      Child Taken Away from Parents for Medical Reasons Dies in Foster Care 21
      Mother Forced to Give Son Chemo, Even Though He is in Remission 21
      State of Michigan Sues Parents to Force Chemo on Cancer-free Child 21
      Gulf War Vet and Wife Lose Children to CPS because Doctor Prescribed Medical Marijuana for Headaches .. 21
   MedicalKidnap.com is Born 21
      The Diegel Sisters of Phoenix 22
   Medical Kidnapping Stories: Families Speak Out 24
      Alabama 25
      Alaska 29
      Arizona 30
      Arkansas 36
      California 38
      Colorado 51
      Connecticut 52
      Florida 54
      Illinois 55
      Indiana 60
      Kansas 62
      Kentucky 63
      Louisiana 69
      Maine 70
      Maryland 72

Massachusetts 74
Michigan 76
Missouri 82
New York 84
North Carolina 85
Ohio 90
Oklahoma 93
Oregon 96
Pennsylvania 98
South Carolina 100
South Dakota 104
Tennessee 106
Texas 109
Vermont 113
Virginia 114

1st Amendment Rights: Making the Public Aware of the Medical Kidnapping Issue 118
   Child Trafficking in the United States: A Huge Business 119

Chapter 2: Medical Kidnapping in the U.S. – Kidnapping Children for Drug Trials 121
   There is a Shortage of Children for Drug Research Studies 122
   CPS Violates Parental Consent and Freedom of Speech 125
   CPS Collects Federal Funds for Trafficking Children .127
   CPS and Medical Kidnapping 128
   CPS Does Not Help Families, But Destroys Them 129
   Congresswoman Spoke Out Against CPS Abuses Before her Murder 131
   It's Now All about "What is Best for the Child" – Not the Family 132
   U.S. House of Representatives Investigates Medical Trials of Foster Children 134
   Congress Knows Children are being Abused in the CPS System 136
   Advocates for Parental Rights Blow the Whistle on Drug Trial Abuses 138

Conclusion: CPS and Doctors are Kidnapping Children for Medical Research 140
Chapter 3: Are New Pediatric "Child Abuse Specialists" Causing an Increase in Medical Kidnappings? 144
   New Pediatric Subspecialty: the "Child Abuse Pediatrician" 149
   Children's Hospitals Build Entire Teams focused on Child Abuse 150
   Child Abuse is Not A Medical Diagnosis, but a Legal Accusation 151
   Multiple Ethical Concerns for Child Abuse Specialists and Teams 153
   "Defensive Doctoring" Leading to Families Wrongly Accused? 155
   Child Abuse Pediatricians a Self-fulfilling Prophecy? . 156
   Video Surveillance Violates Privacy Rights, Heightens Antagonism 157
   Families Irreparably Damaged, Reputations and Jobs Lost, Children Emotionally Devastated 158
Chapter 4: From Child Protection to State-sponsored Child Kidnapping: How Did we Get Here? 159
   Childhood in Ancient Times often 'Nightmarish' 160
   Western Europe Leads World In Care for Children 161
   'Parens Patriae' Establishes Government as "Ultimate Parent" 162
   Charitable Groups and Local/State Involvement 162
   A New Idea: Children Belong to Society First, Not Family 163
   Pediatrician Spotlights Abuse, All States Required to Establish CPS 166
   Warnings Surface Over Unlimited Powers of Government Child Protection 167
   The Modern, Federally-Funded CPS State Is Born 168
   Federal Focus Shifts from Family Reunification to Adoption 168
   The State Owns Your Children: The Ever-Expanding Arms of CPS and Parens Patriae 169
   CPS Continues to Assert New Reasons for Child Removal 171

    Parents Without Clear Rights – CPS Can Regulate and Control Almost Anything 173
Chapter 5: Does the State Ever Have a "Right" to Remove Children from a Home? 175
    The Bill of Rights...177
    Due Process of Law – Criminal Justice 178
    Is it Legal to Forceably Remove Children from Their Parents Against their Will? 180
    Why is Due Process of Law Not Followed by Child Protection Services?..183
    Attorneys are Fighting Back...185
    Advice to Parents and Families: Know Your Constitutional Rights!..186
    How Do We Define Parental Rights?...........................190
        Two Case Studies..191
    Who Will Stand up for Parental Rights? 195
Chapter 6: A Tribute to Senator Nancy Schaefer – Exposing State-sponsored Kidnappings.........................197
    One of Nancy Schaefer's Last Interviews 201
        Part 1 202
        Part 2 203
        Part 3 204
    The Corrupt Business of Child Protective Services 207
References 221

Acknowledgments

This book is a collaborative effort between myself, as editor and one of the authors of Health Impact News and MedicalKidnap.com, and my staff of writers: Terri LaPoint, John P. Thomas, Monica Mears, Susan Parker, Dale Theresa, Merrie Welch, and others. Terri LaPoint is one of the founders and the assistant editor of MedicalKidnap.com.

Tammi Stefano of the National Safe Child Show has also been instrumental in exposing medical kidnapping via her talk show on UBN radio and TV, and the National Safe Child organization has worked together with us to bring national coverage to this terrible problem.

Others have asked not be mentioned due to the sensitive nature of this material, and the opposition we face from those who would like to silence us.

We have been threatened on numerous occasions, and many family court judges have ordered us, via the parents involved in the kidnapping cases, to remove our stories. We have frequently been the focus of very sophisticated attacks against our website servers, but thank God we have continued to expose this corruption in our nation that is ripping families apart.

As long as the first amendment to the Constitution of the United States of America remains in force, protecting freedom of speech and freedom of the press, we will continue publishing these stories.

I am currently of sound mind and good health, with no suicidal thoughts, so any news of my untimely death should be viewed with suspicion.

Brian Shilhavy
Editor, Health Impact News

Chapter 1 – Medical Kidnapping: A Threat to Every Child in America Today

If you live in the United States of America today, and you have children in your home under the age of 18, every day you are in danger of losing your children to the State through medical kidnapping. Something as simple as bringing your child to the local emergency room to care for an injury or sickness puts you at risk for being accused of medically abusing or neglecting your child, and having a doctor direct a social worker to remove the child or children from your custody by force.

Since launching MedicalKidnap.com in late 2014, we have published dozens of such stories in which parents lost custody of their child or children, simply because a medical professional deemed them unworthy parents. Medical kidnapping is defined as the state taking away children from their parents and putting them into state custody and the foster care system, simply because the parents did not agree with a doctor regarding their prescribed medical treatment for the family. In some cases it is as simple as telling a doctor you are going to seek a second opinion on a suggested medical procedure, and then ending up being charged with "medical abuse" and losing your children.

Medical kidnapping is part of a larger problem of state-sponsored child kidnapping. State-sponsored kidnapping is where the state steps in and decides that they know what is best for a child or group of children within a family, and then removes the children without any formal charges being brought against the parents. The parents lose their children immediately, often without any warrant being issued by a judge. They are assumed guilty by social services of something worthy of losing their children, usually with no formal charges filed in a court of law, and no trial by a jury of peers as is afforded by the Constitution of the United States of America. They must spend significant resources to try to get their children back from a family court system that is cloaked in secrecy with little to no accountability. Sometimes the parents are able to get their children back, but sometimes they do not, and the children are adopted out. Even in the instances in which the children are allowed to return home to their parents, they are severely traumatized.

Therefore, much of what we describe and document in this book can also be applied to state-sponsored kidnappings in general, and not just medical kidnapping.

While we have published over 400 articles on the medical kidnapping issue in just a little over a year's time, we have good reason to believe that the family stories we have published represent but a mere fraction of the tragic stories currently happening all across America today. Every day heart-broken parents contact us looking for help, but very few are willing to go public with their stories. They fear the state, because they hold their children, and they want to believe that if they just do what the state tells them to do, they will get their children back. Usually the ones willing to go public have already spent many weeks or months fighting a corrupt system, one that has little to no accountability, and they have given up hope. They want the public to know their story. They want to warn others. When they do go public, the judge over their case in family court usually issues a gag order against them. Many attorneys around the country have stated that these gag orders are unconstitutional.

Also, since we are one of the few news organizations to tackle this issue, many have now also started to come to us with adult medical kidnapping issues, including the kidnapping of seniors and the seizure of their assets to cover medical expenses. We are beginning to investigate and report on these stories as well.

Medical Kidnapping is Real

We have been covering medical kidnapping stories at Health Impact News since the year Health Impact News started, in 2011. The first stories we published were stories that were originally published by local mainstream media in the communities where the medical kidnappings allegedly occurred. Here are a few of the original stories we covered before MedicalKidnap.com was started.

The Godboldo Family of Detroit

Maryanne Godboldo with a picture of her daughter Arianna.

In 2011 we were one of the first national media outlets to cover the Maryanne Godboldo story, which was first picked up by the local Detroit Free Press. Maryanne Godboldo, a Detroit homeschooling mother who refused to give her child powerful antipsychotic drugs after she was developmentally disabled due to vaccine injuries, refused to give up her daughter to Child Protection Services, so they called in a S.W.A.T. team and had Maryanne arrested, and seized her daughter. It was one of our top stories in 2011.

Maryanne Godboldo's story is told in the following video:

https://youtu.be/6hIlo7KD2L0

This long protracted legal battle, which has resulted in the child being reunited with her mother and all charges against the mother dropped, would not have been possible without Attorney Allison Folmar.

https://youtu.be/Cz7CJ1bYioM

In January of 2016, the Michigan Court of Appeals reversed her dismissal and remanded the matter back to the district court. So her legal battle continues.

The Nikolayev Family of Sacramento

Anna and Alex Nikolayev with their baby Sammy.

The second major medical kidnapping story that Health Impact News covered was in 2013 - the story of the

Nikolayev family in Sacramento. This story came to our attention only because local media in Sacramento picked it up, and it was highly publicized.

Anna and Alex Nikolayev's baby Sammy was seized by Child Protection Services, with the help of local law enforcement, simply because they took their baby to a different hospital to get a second opinion about heart surgery. The entire incident where the child was removed by force was captured on video:

https://youtu.be/Pr1ID0CwpBU

In the unedited video above, the entire incident of Child Protective Services and the Sacramento Police using force to take away Anna and Alex Nikolayev's baby is recorded. Anna and Alex had received poor care for their baby at a local hospital, and when the hospital wanted to do heart surgery on their infant, they wanted a second opinion and took the baby to a different hospital.

The first hospital did not approve of this and did not discharge the child. Therefore, they called Child Protection Services. The parents, meanwhile, had taken the baby to a second hospital, where the child was discharged that night by a physician, since there was no immediate danger, and the surgery was not imminent.

But, the next day, Child Protection Services and the Sacramento Police showed up at the parents' home to take away their baby. The husband was outside at the time, and he was forced to the ground so that the police could enter the home by force. The mother, seeing what was happening outside, set up the camera to record the whole incident (see video above). The social workers would not even tell the mother where they were taking the baby.

The police took the baby out of the mother's arms by force, and only after the social workers had already left with the baby did they allow the mother to show the hospital documents showing that their baby was properly discharged by a physician from the second hospital. The police did not seem to care what the facts were at all, and gave full authority to CPS to remove the child. (Full story: http://healthimpactnews.com/2013/cps-assaults-father-and-snatches-baby-from-mother-after-doctor-discharges-baby-from-hospital/)

Senior Consul of Russia, Vycheslav Uvarov, in San Francisco in the court in Sacramento, with Honorary Consul of Russia, Natalia Owen. Photo by Alexander Klimov - posted on Facebook.

Since the father is a Russian national, this incident caused an international uproar. Russia accused the United States of abusing the couple's human rights. Diplomats were sent to attend the hearing in Sacramento. (Full story here: http://healthimpactnews.com/2013/tables-turned-russia-complains-of-human-rights-abuse-in-the-u-s-with-cps-case-in-sacramento/)

Fox News covered the story nationally, and you can see one of their reports on former California Assemblyman Tim Donnelly's YouTube channel.

https://www.youtube.com/watch?v=Yf3dEPB1NjM

The Rider Family of Kansas City

Michelle Rider and her 16-year-old son, Isaiah Rider, traveled from Kansas City to Lurie Children's Hospital in Chicago after doctors in her hometown, Texas, and Boston were unable to effectively treat his neurofibromatosis — a painful condition that causes tumors to grow on his nerves. When Isaiah's pain was reportedly not getting any better at Lurie, his mother attempted to have him transferred to another hospital.

But doctors at Lurie Children's Hospital reported to Cook County Court that Michelle was guilty of "medical child abuse," as they disagreed with the course of treatment chosen by the mother. As a result, they seized custody of Isaiah and put him into a foster home in a rough neighborhood in Chicago, where he claims he was sexually abused.

We only knew about this story because the local media in Kansas City picked up the story. Learn more about Isaiah Rider's story which continues today:
http://medicalkidnap.com/tag/isaiah-rider/

Justina Pelletier and Boston Children's Hospital

In 2013 and 2014, Justina Pelletier became a national symbol for children and families all across America who have gone through medical kidnapping. The Pelletier family is from Connecticut, and a local reporter from Connecticut, Beau Berman, first reported on the story.

When Justina was finally released from state custody after national outrage, Justina and her family traveled to Washington D.C. to promote "Justina's Law," a bipartisan bill proposed to end medical research on children. She received a standing ovation from members of Congress.

Justina was taken away from her parents by force at the age of 15, and held for over a year as Boston Children's Hospital kept her confined in their psych ward. They disagreed with the family's doctor over her diagnosis, and had the state's "child protection" social service agency seize custody of her away from her parents, against her will and the will of her parents. What ensued was a long legal battle to get their daughter back, that probably only ended positively because her story went viral and was picked up by the national mainstream media, because her father refused to obey a court-directed gag order and went to the media with their story. Media heavyweights such as Dr. Phil, Mike Huckabee, and Glenn Beck picked up her story.

Here is a plea Justina made herself to Governor Patrick and Judge Johnston just before she was finally released:

https://youtu.be/20xv15LsVjw

For many Americans, Justina's story was their first exposure to the medical kidnapping issue, since it was reported so widely by national media personalities. However, Justina's case was neither unique nor rare, and what happened to her and her family has happened to many thousands of other children and families all across the United States.

Other stories that Health Impact News reported on because other media outlets first reported the stories include:

Family of Amish Girl Who Fled the Country to Avoid Forced Experimental Chemo Tells Their Side of the Story

http://healthimpactnews.com/2013/family-of-amish-girl-who-fled-the-country-to-avoid-forced-experimental-chemo-tells-their-side-of-the-story/

Child Taken Away from Parents for Medical Reasons Dies in Foster Care

http://healthimpactnews.com/2013/child-taken-away-from-parents-for-medical-reasons-dies-in-foster-care/

Mother Forced to Give Son Chemo, Even Though He is in Remission

http://healthimpactnews.com/2013/mother-forced-to-give-son-chemo-even-though-he-is-in-remission/

State of Michigan Sues Parents to Force Chemo on Cancer-free Child

http://healthimpactnews.com/2011/state-of-michigan-sues-parents-to-force-chemo-on-cancer-free-child/

Gulf War Vet and Wife Lose Children to CPS because Doctor Prescribed Medical Marijuana for Headaches

http://healthimpactnews.com/2013/gulf-war-vet-and-wife-lose-children-to-cps-because-doctor-prescribed-medical-marijuana-for-headaches/

MedicalKidnap.com is Born

Late in 2014, Health Impact News was receiving so many reports from parents who were telling us their stories about how their children were being medically kidnapped, that we started a separate website just to document their stories.

Most of them had nowhere else to go, as they did not have the advantage of any local media picking up their story. Many of the stories that we began to publish on behalf of the families were originally reported by us, and then later picked up by local mainstream media after the story went viral on the Internet and through social media.

The Diegel Sisters of Phoenix

In a case bearing several similarities to Justina Pelletier's family's experience with Boston Children's Hospital, and Isaiah Rider's family's experience with Lurie Children's Hospital in Chicago, 10 and 12 year old sisters were seized by Phoenix Children's Hospital over a medical dispute. The mother was reportedly ordered not to discuss the case with anyone, and forced to take down YouTube videos and a Facebook Page with over 3000 followers that was documenting the actions of Child Protection Services and doctors at Phoenix Children's Hospital.

Kayla and Hannah Diegel suffer from Congenital Disorder of Glycosylation, (CDG, a form of mitochondrial disease). Part of their condition is also suffering with "gastroparesis," which is a partially paralyzed stomach. As a result, they were fed through feeding tubes to bypass the stomach.

During the course of their treatment, the girls' family doctor's clinic of eight years, Estrella Mountain Medical Group, suddenly sent a letter to the parents instructing them to transfer the girls to the care of Phoenix Children's Hospital Special Needs Clinic. They bounced between several different doctors at PCH, but they were all in the field of genetics. It was during this time that the girls were diagnosed with "Congenital Disorder of Glycosylation" (CDG).

Unknown to the parents at the time, funding and drug trials were going on for this rare condition. The article on the Facebook Page reports: "The glycosylation trial whose collaborative agreement is through NHGRI/TGEN opened up on March 14th, 2014, just 3 weeks before the two Phoenix sisters were medically kidnapped."

The mother reportedly began to suspect that something was going on, as she reviewed the medical records and medications her daughters were receiving. She requested that the care of her daughters be transferred to another doctor "due to his neglect and endangerment of younger daughter i.e., not returning phone calls, ignoring her severe pain and documented bowel impaction being treated from home by registered nurses, under his supervision."

Shortly after this, in April of 2014, the hospital took custody of both daughters away from the family through CPS. Health Impact News was ordered by the court in Arizona, via Melissa Diegel, to remove their story (Health Impact News did not comply).

Medical Kidnapping Stories: Families Speak Out

After the Diegel family story, many more started pouring in through MedicalKidnap.com. More stories are reported to us each day than we are able to publish. We verify each story we investigate, usually speaking with family members, attorneys, and others associated with each case. Many times, the family backs out at the last minute, fearful of reprisal by those who hold their children. Often, local media will also pick up the story and do their own interviews.

We allow the families to tell their story to the public. The state agencies who abduct the children will not comment on specific stories. What they do is veiled in secrecy within family or juvenile court systems, and very seldom will parents actually be arrested or charged with any crimes in a regular court in these cases. Instead, the alleged victims, the children, are incarcerated within the foster care system, being ripped away from their families. Massive federal and state funding allow these children to be a financial asset to the state that abducts them.

Here are a few stories we have covered on MedicalKidnap.com, listed by state. Go to MedicalKidnap.com to read the full story.

Alabama

Alabama Girl Medically Kidnapped and Forced on Drugs: Parents Facing Jail for Failure to Pay State Child Support

An Alabama girl has been medically kidnapped from her family because her mother refused to allow social workers to put her daughter on strong antidepressant drugs. The mother had good reason to refuse these drugs, as both of her parents had been prescribed antidepressants by the very same facility - her mother at the age of 22, and her father at age 54, one year prior to the social worker's demand. Both of her parents subsequently committed suicide after taking the medications.

Now, the mother is facing a jail sentence for failing to pay child support to the state for the daughter they kidnapped, and her fiancé has a warrant out for his arrest as well. Due to rumors of corruption and violence in DeKalb County jail, they are terrified for his well-being if he goes to jail, and they are calling on the public for support.

Alabama Autistic Boys Kidnapped from Native American Ambassador Mother and Abused in Foster Care

Just three hours after a Native American mother got home from the hospital after a suspected heart attack, Child Protective Services (known in Alabama as DHR, Department of Human Resources) showed up on her doorstep and took away her two autistic sons. Now, her two sons are living in a foster home in Mobile, almost 250 miles away from their Sylacauga home, and their mother says that they are being abused in foster care and that their culture is being trampled by the social workers and foster parents.

Dawn "Adaleha" ("my sunshine" in Cherokee) Cullins was appointed as the Alabama Ambassador for the Sokoki tribe, and in 2003, was recognized for "acts of compassion and kindness" and awarded the Civic Recognition Award in her community. She holds a degree in Paralegal studies and is very active in tribal activities. Her record is squeaky clean, without so much as a traffic ticket.

DHR got involved with her family after one of her autistic sons wandered away from home and was reported to DHR by neighbors. The charges against her were "a messy house and dirty children."

Today, Dawn claims her children are beaten in foster care, and are given multiple drugs (without her approval) to keep them compliant. She calls it "genocidal kidnapping," and reports that when she told DHR that her children were Native American, the social workers told her that she would never get her kids back.

Alabama Seizes 7 Children from Family After Child with Autism Wandered to Neighbors

An Alabama couple is afraid that they may never get their children back. All 7 of their children were taken by DHR (the state's child protective services) after their not-yet diagnosed child with autism began wandering off. It is called "elopement" in the autism community, and is very common in children diagnosed with autism, happening in 49% of these kids, even in the best of homes and the most carefully guarded of situations. It is scary, but experts say that it does not at all reflect poor parenting.

It has now been over a year since Sabrina and Tony Cartee's children were taken, and the state plans to file to terminate their parental rights for all of their kids, including the baby who was born in September, after the other children were taken by DHR. The breastfeeding newborn was seized at only a day and a half old and placed in a foster home.

Alaska

Medical Kidnap: It Happens to Adults Too

Bret Bohn's family wants the public to know that it is not just children who are being medically kidnapped, being used as medical research lab rats, forced to take drugs, and being kept isolated from their families. They say it happened to their son, too. He was 26 years old at the time.

What began simply enough ended up in an 8 month long nightmare. Bret's mother Lorraine Phillips told Health Impact News that it was "medical torture" and a "horrific abuse of Government corruption and power."

Arizona

Corruption and Medical Malpractice Cover-up involving Arizona CPS - How One Family was Destroyed

Since Health Impact News started publishing stories from families telling about their horrible experiences with medical kidnapping, we have had more families contact us from Arizona than almost all the other states combined.

But one case stands out from all of them in terms of the depth of the corruption in the medical system, and Child Protection Services, within the state of Arizona. Award-winning investigative journalist, Jennifer Margulis, looked into one civil rights case that is currently in the 9th Circuit Court, and found what appears to be a tangled web of corruption and deception in Arizona that will shock you.

Read the story of Darrell and Leanna Smith, and how they lost 2 of their 3 children when Leanna questioned doctors in what appears to be a medical malpractice case. Their family was destroyed, and they are still in the midst of years of legal battles.

How many other families in Arizona do they represent?

Phoenix Children's Hospital Seizes 8 Year Old Boy Because Mother Seeks Second Opinion

Tonya Brown is "just a mom who is in love with her kid," adorable 8-year-old Christopher Reign. Because Tonya questioned a very risky, painful procedure for her son, Tonya reports that his doctor at Phoenix Children's Hospital enlisted Child Protective Services to take him away from her custody.

If the doctor has her way, Tonya could lose her beloved child forever in the upcoming hearings to permanently sever her parental rights later this month – all because a mother wanted to try less invasive options for her son before going to a treatment that carries sizable risks.

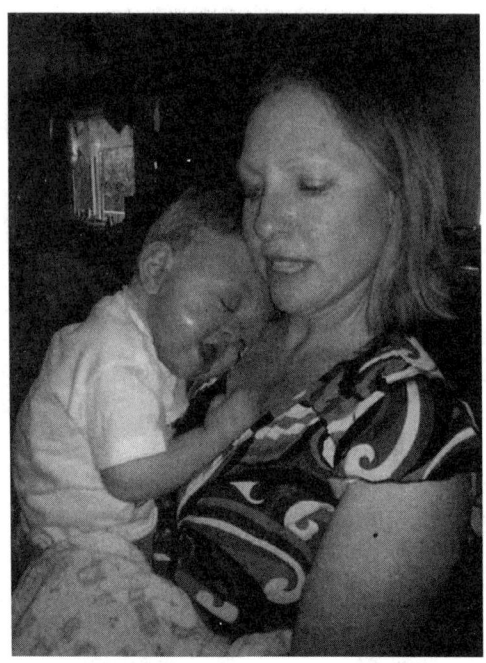

Mom of 2 Year Old Special-Needs Child Asked for Help: Arizona CPS Took Him Away Instead

Lisa Meltzer is an Arizona mom of a special-needs little boy. She and her family received special training to care for this precious little baby.

But one day Lisa was so sick, she felt she needed more help than her family could supply for her son for a short time, while she recovered from her sickness. She called the Arizona State social services to request help.

But according to Lisa, instead of helping, they removed the child from her custody and are now offering him up for adoption to foster parents. Even though she has not been charged with abuse, the state apparently believes they can remove the child simply based on his complicated medical needs. Her parental rights have allegedly been violated, as she has not been able to visit her 2 year old son for 4 months, and the Arizona Attorney General and Family Court Judge allegedly removed her from court when she tried to speak up for her parental rights.

What is going on in Arizona?

Arizona CPS Takes 7 Children Away from Parents after Accident

The unthinkable happened to a family in Arizona. Their three-year-old daughter mysteriously collapsed while her parents were away from home, and she died shortly after. As horrible as that tragedy was, Khloe's death was only the beginning of the devastation to the Shoars family. Child Protective Services immediately came in and took away all seven of their other children, placing them in various foster home settings around the area.

The children now don't have their parents, or even each other, as they try to grasp what has happened to their sister. None of the children, ranging in age from 2 to 9 years old, have been placed with family or friends, and they cry to come home. They don't understand what has happened, and neither do their parents, Jeff and Tabitha Shoars.

"It's like a bad nightmare you can't wake up from," says Jeff.

No charges have been filed against anyone, yet the State of Arizona has already begun the TPR process, Termination of Parental Rights.

10 and 12 Year Old Sisters Seized from Family by Hospital in Phoenix

In a case bearing several similarities to Justina Pelletier's family's experience with Boston Children's Hospital, and Isaiah Rider's family's experience with Lurie Children's Hospital in Chicago, 10 and 12 year old sisters have been seized by Phoenix Children's Hospital over a medical dispute. The mother has reportedly been ordered not to discuss the case with anyone, and has been forced to take down YouTube videos and a Facebook Page with over 3000 followers that was documenting the actions of Child Protection Services and doctors at Phoenix Children's Hospital.

Kayla and Hannah Diegel suffer from Congenital Disorder of Glycosylation, (CDG, a form of mitochondrial disease). Part of their condition is also suffering with "gastroparesis," which is a partially paralyzed stomach. As a result, they were fed through feeding tubes to bypass the stomach.

During the course of their treatment, the girls' family doctor's clinic of eight years, Estrella Mountain Medical Group, suddenly sent a letter to the parents instructing them to transfer the girls to the care of Phoenix Children's Hospital Special Needs Clinic. They bounced between several different doctors at PCH, but they were all in the field of genetics. It was during this time that the girls were diagnosed with "Congenital Disorder of Glycosylation" (CDG).

Unknown to the parents at the time, funding and drug trials were going on for this rare condition. The article on the Facebook Page reports: "The glycosylation trial whose collaborative agreement is through NHGRI/TGEN opened up on March 14th, 2014, just 3 weeks before the two Phoenix sisters were medically kidnapped."

The mother reportedly began to suspect that something was going on, as she reviewed the medical records and medications her daughters were receiving. She requested that the care of her daughters be transferred to another doctor "due to his neglect and endangerment of younger daughter i.e., not returning phone calls, ignoring her severe pain and documented bowel impaction being treated from home by registered nurses, under his supervision."

Shortly after this, in April of 2014, the hospital took custody of both daughters away from the family through CPS.

The family contends that the daughters are suffering since being removed from their family, as their feeding tubes have been removed. Kayla has reportedly lost 25% of her body weight after being in the custody of PCH for four months.

Arkansas

Arkansas Takes Away 7 Homeschooled Children

Relatives of the Stanley family in Garland County, Arkansas have reached out to MedicalKidnap.com to notify the public that the 7 homeschooled children of Hal and Michelle Stanley were removed during the night by DHS and fully armed sheriffs this past week, simply because they reportedly found a supplement in the home that was not approved by the FDA.

The mother sent an emotional email to family and friends describing what happened. Some quotes:

"It was freezing cold and neither Hal nor I had on coats. After stepping outside they issued us a search warrant and said we could not enter our house or talk to our kids until the search and the investigation was through. We could not go get a coat; we could not call a lawyer; we could not retrieve anything inside like a phone or a camera to record anything or call anyone. It was almost 30 minutes later before they retrieved our coats for us to put on."

"The call was anonymous and therefore the caller was protected while all our rights were taken away. We of course expressed all our concerns as to what this would do to the kids since they've never been to the doctor for sickness or health issues and they've never been away from us in that type of setting."

"All the little kids were upset and Hal and I and the girls were all crying and in shock. When I did calm down for the kids' sake, and try to comfort them they ripped them away from us saying that we had already taken too much time and that they had to go. I still can't believe they are gone. I have no idea what will happen tomorrow or what comes next."

If you currently have any supplement or non-pharmaceutical product in your home that you are using to treat a sickness or disease, they could come for your kids next.

California

Medically Kidnapped Disabled Man Held Against his Will in Orange County California

Nate Tseglin was born on November 5, 1989 to Ilya and Riva Tsleglin. The parents, now residents of California, are originally from the former Soviet Union. They have a younger son Robert as well.

Nate was diagnosed with Asperger's syndrome at age 14. He was first taken away from his parents by the State of California on January 12, 2007 at age 17 when a teacher reported his parents to the Child Protective Services (CPS) because Nate was scratching himself on the arms. His family has been fighting for him to be home, and to be cared for at home, ever since. He is currently being detained by the State of California against his own will, and also the will of his family. Nate is now an adult. He is allegedly being forced to take drugs his family does not approve, and is kept locked up like a prisoner.

The Tseglin family would like the public to know their story of medical kidnapping happening in California. They do not believe that having a disability such as Asperger's syndrome gives the state a right to kidnap their son.

UCLA Medical Doctors and LA County Medically Kidnap Paramedic and Film Producer's Daughter

Tammi Stefano of The National Safe Child Show recently interviewed Jewels Stein, a mother who had her daughter taken by Los Angeles County's Department of Child and Family Services (DCFS) following accusations of Munchausen by proxy by UCLA medical physicians.

Jewels Stein is a paramedic with the Fire Department who has an extensive medical background. She works on movie sets, and she is currently producing a documentary. She raised four of her own children and two stepchildren.

On the day her 15 year old daughter was to be discharged from the hospital after a successful surgery that allowed her daughter to eat food again instead of being fed by a tube inserted directly into her stomach, Jewels Stein watched in horror as they took her daughter away from her because she refused to let her be put on powerful psych drugs. She was escorted out of the hospital while still in her pajamas, and left on the street without even her car keys.

This is her story that she wants the world to hear.

Medically Kidnapped Child in LA County DCFS Care Dies – Father Vows to Expose Criminal Social Workers

A report written about LA County Department of Children and Family Services (DCFS) revealed that during an 18 month period, of the thousands of children who were taken away from their parents and family members, 571 of them died while under the supervision of LA County DCFS.

On Sunday September 28, 2015 Jason Janbahan appeared on the National Safe Child show to tell his story of how a corrupt social service agency in LA County was responsible for the kidnapping and death of his 5 year old son. Having his son removed from his home due to a charge of "medical neglect," in spite of the fact that medical reports showed that his son was in normal health, once under the care of a foster mother in a group home, the 5 year old boy's fragile immune system deteriorated rapidly, and he died while in the custody of LA County DCFS.

Los Angeles County DCFS Horror Story: Baby Kidnapped for Two Years and Innocent Mother Incarcerated

Tammi Stefano interviewed Amy Duran on Friday, August 28th on The National Safe Child Show. Amy is a mother who had her son taken by Los Angeles County's Department of Child and Family Services (DCFS) with the help of the Police Department. Vindictive people used DCFS and local law enforcement to kidnap Amy's son, and to put Amy into a holding cell in a detention center where she was told she would spend the next 12 years, even though she had violated no laws and was not convicted of any crimes. During this time, Amy fainted several times, and could not tell the difference between night and day as there were no windows in the cell.

Amy never gave up, however. She fought back, and over three and a half years later she won her case and had her son returned to her custody. Her son was kidnapped by DCFS when he was 11 months old, and at age 4 he has now spent more than half of his life away from his mother and in foster care with strange people.

Here is Amy's story, showing an example of how LA County DCFS does not protect children, but destroys families.

Harvard-trained Beverly Hills Doctor Mom Has 4 Children Kidnapped by LA County DCFS

Dr. Susan Evans graduated from Harvard Medical School with dual medical degrees in dermatology and internal medicine. She established her medical practice specializing in dermatology in the heart of Beverly Hills, CA. Most of her clientele are celebrities we only see on the big screen. Along with the limelight clientele, Dr. Susan's expertise has been sought as a medical expert on Dr. Oz, Oprah, the Doctors, CNN, the TODAY show and many more.

Dr. Susan is the mother of four children: 10 year old twin daughters, L. Elizabeth, S. Mary, and two sons, Nick, age

14 and Z. Hugh, age 8. She was voted Dr. Mom on the TV series Dr. 90210.

However, like thousands of other parents in Los Angeles County, she has lost her 4 children to LA County Department of Child and Family Services (DCFS), even though no charges have ever been filed against her. Not only have no charges been filed against her, a dependency court judge ruled that there was no reason for DCFS to keep her children out of her custody, and dismissed the case with prejudice (meaning the evidence they presented could not be brought before the dependency court again).

So, why is she still battling LA County DCFS to get her children back? How has a child "protection" social services agency like LA County DCFS become so powerful, that a respected medical doctor from the affluent Beverly Hills community is rendered helpless over what she believes is the state-sponsored kidnapping of her children?

CPS Threatens To Kidnap 7 Year Old in California When Parents Try to Transfer to Different Hospital

Kennedy May Willey suffered her first seizure shortly after receiving the DTaP vaccine. Today she is a 7 year-old girl diagnosed with Dravet syndrome who has led a very active and "normal" life. They attribute much of their success to the GAPS diet.

When her seizures recently increased, her parents found themselves in a hospital with what they believe was an overzealous doctor who wanted to try a drug cocktail of treatments. Seeing her condition quickly deteriorate, they sought to transfer her to another facility. They were threatened with losing their daughter to CPS, so they hired attorneys to help them get her transferred.

The Willeys want to share their story with others as a warning about the dangers of medical kidnapping so many other parents are facing today. Have we now come to the point in the United States that in order to get one's child transferred to another hospital or seek different treatment options one needs to hire attorneys to do so? What about those who cannot afford attorneys?

Medical Kidnapping in San Bernardino California: Innocent Mom Goes To Jail?

September 4, 2013, a San Bernardino County social worker instructed the mother of two-year-old Melina to "pack up her daughters stuff…she belongs to the county now."

Heavenly Ramos of Upland California, the mother of Melina, had her daughter removed from her home based on allegations that she had 5 bone fractures, all with different levels of healing, throughout her body.

Christopher McCown, who had been with Heavenly and little Melina since she was two months old, raced home after a 2 hour interrogation by CPS, but he was moments too late. In tears, Heavenly recalls him saying,

"I didn't even get to say good bye…they took her and I couldn't even tell her how much I love her."

Eleven months after that day, CPS removed their other child, newborn son, Jacob, hours after his birth. The couple now has no children left at home.

California Holds Medically Kidnapped Adult Daughter for 14 Years

Jeffrey and Elsie Golin have been fighting against the State of California and California's San Andreas Regional Center (SARC) for nearly fifteen years to have their daughter returned to them. SARC is a community-based, private nonprofit corporation funded by the State of California and working with Stanford University to serve people with developmental disabilities. The Golins are fighting for their autistic daughter Nancy's right to be able to return home to live with them, and fighting for the right to advocate for their daughter's best interests.

According to their main attorney, Dave Beauvais, there are two main issues that lie at the heart of this ongoing case. The first is the issue of the Golin's losing all rights to act in their own daughter Nancy's best interests and the second is the issue of whether a person who is disabled has the same protection under the U.S. Constitution as a non-disabled person does.

The two issues the state brought as grounds for removing Nancy from their care were the fact that she wanders away and the fact that the Golins disagreed with the doctors at Stanford University about which medication was best to prevent Nancy's seizures.

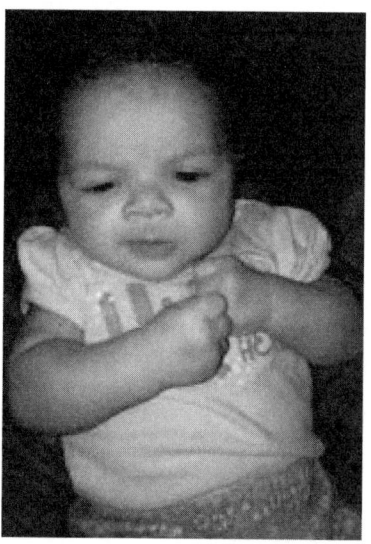

California Parents Blamed for SIDS Death – Lose Remaining Children to CPS

Crystal Avenger of El Dorado, California states that 3-month old Alana Jo received a Hepatitis B vaccination in the hospital shortly before her death. Approximately one week prior to her death, in March 2015 they took her back to the hospital for a sick visit and she was diagnosed with a common cold.

On the morning of March 18, 2015, Christopher awoke and noticed his daughter, Alana, didn't look normal. His voice was laden with emotion as he recalled,

"I picked her up from the bed and her arms went completely limp."

He immediately called 911 and frantically followed the operator's instructions for CPR on his baby. The other children were watching in horror as Christopher tried desperately to revive Alana. The baby was taken away in an ambulance, and her mother Crystal was not even allowed to go with her.

An investigation began, and despite there being no evidence of abuse by the parents, the remaining four children were removed from the home by force, screaming as they were ripped away from their parents.

California Mother Fights Corrupt System in LA to Get Daughter Back

Not being informed of court hearings. Falsified drug tests. Threats and accusations to intimidate and coerce. Social workers, her state representative and even the attorney assigned to her case ignoring emails, not returning calls. Her daughter ripped from a happy home and placed in a non-English speaking foster home without critical, lifesaving medications. A system that seems to have already decided her family's fate, without even the most cursory attempt at justice.

Mayan Hewes describes these events and wonders what happened to her rights, and the rights of her six-year-old daughter Layla, in LA County, California.

Breastfed Babies Kidnapped by CPS Because Parents were "Homeless" Living out of RV

Amber is one of those free-spirited people who takes even incredible hardships and turns them into adventures, inspiring others in the process. When her young family wound up homeless, through no fault of their own, she and her husband Krishna Mehta made the best of it. Their children didn't even know that they were homeless; they thought that they were having great adventures and making lots of friends.

This latest chapter in their saga, however, is a nightmare, and the rainbow is really hard to find in the storm that Child

Protective Services has brought into their lives. Their children, ages 6, almost 2, and 9 months, have been seized by CPS and placed into 3 different foster homes. The two babies were still being breastfed. Social services has gone so far as to accuse Amber of having a mental disorder because she is "homeless," even though the family RV they were living out of was apparently approved as "acceptable."

Now under state control, Amber says the children are suffering poor health whereas before they were healthy, happy children. She was forced to consent to vaccinations against her wish, under threat of being charged with "medical neglect."

Colorado

Boy Removed from Family – Father Jailed Over Lyme Disease Disagreement

At this time of year, most families are looking forward to the festive season and preparing for Christmas. However, for one family, Christmas is the last thing on their minds. In the space of just a few months, they report how their lives have been torn apart by Child Protective Services (CPS) in Colorado.

Due to an alleged disagreement over a Lyme disease diagnosis, their son has been put into State Custody, the father has served time in jail, and the mother is now in hiding due to fear.

Connecticut

No Charges Filed, But 3-year Old Child with Cancer Taken from Mother over "Diaper Rash"

A little boy recovering from a brain tumor has been taken from his mother, in what some are calling a medical kidnapping in Connecticut. After surviving a year of intensive chemotherapy and radiation treatments, 3 year old Weston Lamarre was declared to be in remission and cancer-free.

But just two months later Child Protective Services stepped in and took him away from the mother who stayed by his side every step of the way on their heartrending journey.

Now Wendy Lamarre is fighting to get her son back.

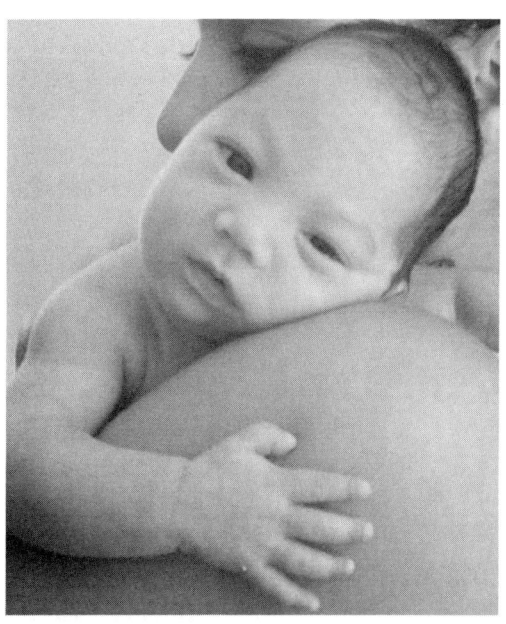

17 Month Old Baby Taken from Family who Disagrees with Doctors

Jessica Gilmore says, "I just want to love my grandson. That's all I want." However, if Connecticut DCF (their child protective services) has their way, little 17-month-old Jaxon Gilmore, who may not have much longer to live, will be adopted out to strangers, all because a grandmother allegedly questioned authority, seeking the best possible care for her sick grandchild.

Florida

Florida Refuses to Return 7 Children to Loving Parents who are Not Accused of Any Crime

While the nation celebrates Independence Day with barbecues, fireworks, and family get-togethers, Freddie and Tracey Verzosa are struggling to maintain hope. Freddie's voice broke as he told Health Impact News that this week, July 9, marks 1 year to the day since their beloved children were ripped away from them by Florida CPS because Tracey has a "mild intellectual disability."

Later, their newborn baby was literally taken from her mother's arms just one day after she was born on March 11, 2015, simply because the state already had custody of the other 6 children.

To date, the parents have never been charged with abuse or neglect, yet the state still has their children. The children are still in various foster homes, separated not only from their parents, but also from each other.

Since Health Impact News broke their heart-wrenching story on the day that baby Taylor Lynn was taken in March, the Verzosas have received a huge outpouring of love and support, but their children remain separated from them.

The father reports that their children were in good health before the state took them, but now there always seems to be something wrong with them. He says that they often look drugged up, and that all the kids except the baby are on some type of medication. Their 8-year old son was also forcibly circumcised against the desires of the parents.

Illinois

Isaiah Rider is 18 Now, but Illinois Maintains Custody of Medically Kidnapped Missouri Teen

Illinois continues to "terrorize" Missouri resident Isaiah Rider and his family, even after he turned 18 last August. The family had hoped that they would leave them alone, but that has not happened. It may not have been in the news lately, but their medical kidnapping story is anything but over.

Isaiah's mother, Michelle Rider, thought that things would settle down after an appellate court said that Illinois DCFS should not be involved after Isaiah's 18th birthday. They thought their nightmare with the Child Protective System was finally over.

However, they have learned that the Cook County Juvenile Court, with the same judge and same players, continues to hold hearings about Isaiah. Usually he and his mother are not informed or invited to these hearings, some of which are off the record, even though it is their lives that are being decided by this entity.

Michelle has learned that the state of Illinois continues to receive federal Title IV-E money for her son. Could this be the reason why Illinois won't let go of their case?

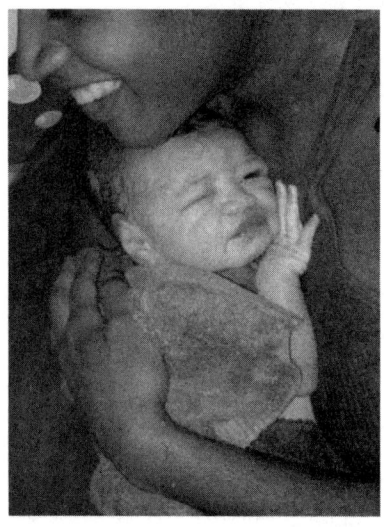

Homebirthed Newborn Medically Kidnapped at Illinois Children's Hospital

The date was May 23, 2012. It was a beautiful midwife-assisted homebirth: a planned water birth and lotus birth. Mother Dontia, father Armondo, big brother Deon, and new baby sister Asaliah, were all happy and doing great after the birth. However, concerns regarding redness around the umbilical cord at Asaliah's navel caused mom to seek medical treatment on June 8, 2012, at the OSF St. Francis Children's Hospital in Peoria, Illinois.

Little did Dontia know that this seemingly unassuming trip to the E.R., seeking help for her baby's infection, would reportedly end up completely destroying her life by removing both her 11 year-old son and her newborn baby from her custody, violating what she claims is her constitutional right to religious freedom, and later, while still in the midst of fighting CPS for her medically kidnapped children, sending her into a life of hiding and secrecy to protect the life of her third yet unborn child.

Deon is now 14, Asaliah is now 3, and her third child (un-named to conceal her identity and protect her from being seized), is now 2. Dontia has not seen or spoken to Deon in three years, nor has she had visitations with Asaliah since she fled Illinois, unable to bear the loss of another child.

Dontia and her third child remain in hiding today.

Chicago Lurie Children's Hospital Takes Baby Away From Family for Seeking a Second Opinion

When Lakisha Tanna's infant grandson was transferred to Lurie Children's Hospital in Chicago, Illinois, she thought that he was in the best place he could be to receive the care that he needed for his medical condition. She never dreamed that this choice would eventually result in her adorable grandchild being what she terms "medically kidnapped" more than a year later.

On March 12, the family faces a hearing to determine whether Malik, now 2 1/2, will be able to return home to his grandparents who love him, or forever become a ward of the state of Illinois.

Another Medical Kidnap in Illinois: Infant Twins Seized from Parents over Medical Dispute

Cassaundra Brown is heartbroken because she is missing her twins' first Christmas. Instead of watching 9 month old Arianna and Dominick delight in the Christmas lights and new toys and pretty bows, she and Warnell Ludington are caught in a desperate fight for their babies with DCFS, the child protective services department in Illinois, over what they believe in their hearts is a misdiagnosis.

Cassaundra says, "I can't even believe this is happening."

The crux of the twins' removal from their parents allegedly lies in an accusation of shaken baby syndrome, a diagnosis which is surrounded by growing skepticism by medical experts, and which does not take into account Arianna's history of medical complications since her birth. Though the parents have reportedly not been charged with any crime, their children have been seized by the state; and they are only permitted to see them for two hours per week.

Their visit this week was canceled because the foster parents are out of town for the Christmas holidays.

This foster home is the twins' fourth foster home in five months.

Their parents are grieving because they are "missing out on every first," and just want their babies back.

Indiana

Indiana Parents' Trip to E.R. Results in Children Kidnapped – Names Slandered in Local Media – Lives Ruined

On June 8th, 2015, Nikki and Rodney Wisler of Anderson, Indiana, noticed bruises on their one-month old daughter Leigh Ann. They took her to Community Hospital Anderson's Emergency Room, as advised by their pediatrician over the phone. The concerned parents worried that their new baby might have a genetic disorder that caused the bruises, since their 2.5 year-old daughter Caridie had been diagnosed with a genetic disorder the previous year.

Initially, the E.R. did not find anything of concern, and since the baby was not in pain, they sent the parents home, advising them to follow up with their regular pediatrician the next morning. The following day, their pediatrician sent the parents back to the hospital for x-rays and a head ultrasound. After they left the hospital, they were called back again for additional x-rays to "rule out a fracture."

Later, the pediatrician called them, saying there was a tibia fracture, and directed them to come back to the E.R. to have the baby's leg splinted. The pediatrician explained that she had to call the Department of Child Services (DCS) because there was an unexplained fracture and bruises. Nikki and Rodney weren't concerned, since they knew they had done nothing wrong. However, they were traumatized when DCS seized custody of their children that night and accused them of abuse.

Without an investigation or even a home visit, warrants were issued for the Wisler's arrest. The Wislers lost everything: their children, their reputations, their jobs, and their home. The Wislers are shocked how the system can be so heartless and punitive towards loving parents, and how the doctors, social workers, and prosecuting attorneys are quick to call "child abuse" and destroy a family without an investigation or any evidence.

Further evidence has shown that there was actually no fracture, and doctors have reversed their opinions on the matter. However, the Wislers are still without their children, and without employment as the community believes they are guilty of child abuse.

Kansas

**Special Needs Sisters Kidnapped From
Homeschooling Christian Family**

Throughout history, people have taken a stand for their faith which oftentimes resulted in unfavorable consequences for the individuals. For disabled veteran David Owen and his wife Teresa, their refusal to stop practicing their Christian faith was ultimately used as a rationale for Kansas Department for Children and Families (DCF) seizing custody of their two special-needs daughters, Angel and Catrina. According to Teresa Owen:

"Our daughters were wrongfully removed from our home because we refused to stop attending church and teaching our daughters about Christ. Angel and Catrina are being wrongfully kept out of our home, abused, and medically neglected. We are still fighting for our daughters and trying to help other families."

Their children were taken at the beginning of 2011. To this day, they are not home, and Teresa and David are fighting to regain custody of their daughters. They believe their daughters are being abused both physically and emotionally in state custody, and are pleading with people to get their story published.

Kentucky

Kentucky Parents Found Not Guilty of Charges in Criminal Court but Family Court Refuses to Return Children

We bring you one Kentucky family's story that illustrates the incredible struggle families face today in what many call an unjust Family Court, and what happens when DCBS relies on unproven allegations.

When Danny and Leeann Foster of Christian County, Kentucky fell on hard times in the summer of 2015, they decided to move to Louisville to look for work. Not finding work there, Danny moved to Nashville, TN to work in his father's business as an electrician, while Leeann and their two daughters, Bailey age 5 and Danica age 2, stayed in

Louisville. Leeann's mother Sonya offered to have the children come stay with her for the summer, and since the children would enjoy summer back in their old hometown better than staying in Louisville, Leeann agreed. Leeann never could have imagined the nightmare that was about to unfold when her own mother would make allegations that she and Danny had sexually abused their own daughters.

There is no argument that physical and sexual child abuse is a crime, and if found guilty in a due process Criminal Court of law, that the criminals should be incarcerated.

But what if you were accused of sexual abuse based on a false allegation and a faulty medical exam, arrested, incarcerated, then released from jail because the Criminal Court dropped the charges for insufficient evidence, yet you learned that Family Court would not return your children because they were still going to press charges? How is it you can be Not Guilty in Criminal Court, but Guilty in Family Court on the same charges? The 5th Amendment says that no person shall be tried for the same offense twice, so it begs the question, is this a type of Double Jeopardy and a way around the 5th Amendment?

Pregnant Homeschool Mom Assaulted by Sheriff as CPS Kidnaps Her Kids in Kentucky

Friends of the Naugler family in Kentucky reached out to us and asked us to tell their story. Their 10 homeschooled children were taken away by Breckinridge County sheriff deputies and CPS this week, allegedly acting on an anonymous tip. The officers reportedly had no warrant to enter their property. Nicole Naugler is currently 5 months pregnant, and reportedly attempted to drive away from the property with a couple of the children. Officers allegedly detained her from leaving her own property, and when she objected to them taking away her children, they allegedly "slammed (her) belly first into the cop car and bruised and scraped both arms."

They also arrested her for "disorderly conduct" when she objected to them taking away her children; and she spent the night in jail. All ten children are reportedly now in state custody. Much of the encounter with CPS and the sheriff deputies was recorded, and the recordings are available on the Save Our Family blog.

Kentucky Baby Medically Kidnapped Along with Siblings and Forced on to Formula

Cody and Ashley Miller of Kentucky took their sick 5-month old baby Easton to the Emergency Room of Monroe Carell Jr. Children's Hospital at Vanderbilt in Nashville, Tennessee late Saturday evening, September 26, 2015. When Vanderbilt made allegations of abuse against these concerned parents, they could barely comprehend what was happening.

Ashley painfully recalled that moment when Shell Peters, the CPS worker (or DCBS in Kentucky) entered the hospital room with 2 officers, and uttered those 2 words: "We're taking…"

Ashley painfully recalls, "My world crumbled when I heard those 2 words. I was nursing Easton one moment, and then they walked in, and then I was balling my eyes out hysterically. He can't be on formula – I'm breastfeeding!"

Medical Kidnapping in Kentucky: Mother Coerced to Give Up Daughter to Adoption in Order to Keep Son

When Brenda Maney of Richmond, KY, walked into her Termination of Parental Rights (TPR) hearing on May 7, 2015, she was not prepared for the impossible choice the Family Court would present to her.

About 2.5 years earlier, in the winter of 2012, a series of unfortunate events in Brenda's life led to a friend naïvely calling Kentucky's Department for Community Based Services (DCBS) for help. DCBS social workers showed up at Brenda's door, and despite the children being well taken care of, removed her children after "diagnosing" her as having postpartum depression and demanding that she check herself into a psychiatric hospital for treatment in order to get her two children back.

Brenda would never get her baby daughter back, despite the fact that she did what DCBS required and checked into the hospital.

At Brenda's TPR hearing, the judge called a recess which lasted about 40 minutes. Brenda's attorney came back and said that the court was offering Brenda a choice – to choose between having her 14-year-old son Aaron come home by giving up her 3-year-old daughter Tanaieah voluntarily to adoption, or lose both children. The attorney explained:

"Your daughter does not know you, she has bonded to the foster family and she is happy. She thinks they are her family. DCBS is going to use her attachment as the 'Best Interest of the Child' and if you continue with the TPR hearing, you will lose. Your son wants to come home. He's miserable in foster care. He's not thriving in foster care. Every potential adoptive home he's been placed in has fallen through. You should take this offer, for Aaron. If you go ahead with the TPR hearing, you will lose. You will lose both children."

Faced with an unbearable likelihood of losing both children, Brenda could not allow Aaron to suffer any longer. Brenda chose to get Aaron out of the foster care system that was destroying him, by relinquishing her rights to Tanaieah. Even though the Family Court required that Brenda sign her rights away "willingly," she did so out of coercion and feeling that she had no other choice.

Louisiana

EXCLUSIVE: State Corruption Exposed in Louisiana High Profile Medical Kidnap Case

Believing his daughter to be innocent, Gerald Price speaks out for the first time in an exclusive interview with Health Impact News on what he says is rampant corruption and collusion in his daughter's high-profile child abuse trial and conviction following a Department of Louisiana Children & Family Services (DCFS) seizure of his grandchildren. DCFS originally refused to award custody of the children to their grandparents, instead putting them into a foster home.

Local media reported the story as if his daughter was already guilty, and she was later convicted and sentenced to 30 years in prison. An appellate court would later vacate that decision and reduce it to 10 years.

Gerald and his wife filed for bankruptcy in the process of fighting for their daughter, and Gerald wrote a book on their whole ordeal: The Darker Side of Justice.

Maine

Medical Kidnapping in Maine: Child with Ehlers-Danlos Syndrome & Sister Seized – Grandfather Commits Suicide

Brandon and Cynthia Ross became concerned after noticing their baby's leg was swollen. Even though Ryder was not crying excessively, had no bruises, red marks, or any outward signs of injury other than the swelling, the couple took him to the doctor for an examination.

After performing some x-rays and finding the infant with multiple fractures throughout his body, the doctors sent the family to the Maine Medical Center (MMC) for further evaluation. Before the couple understood the depths of the evaluation, they were deemed guilty of child abuse by officials at MMC.

Six days after Ryder was admitted to the hospital, the State of Maine chose to remove both Ryder and his two year old sister Rosalynn from their parents' care.

On June 12, 2014, Brandon, their twenty-five year old father, was indicted on twelve counts of child abuse and was arrested by Bath, Maine police. After being transported to the local jail, he received death threats from other inmates. The threats were taken so seriously that the jail provided Brandon with private accommodations for his safety.

On Father's Day of 2014, just days after Brandon's arrest, after telling the family he believed the state was out to get Brandon, Ryder's seventy-four year old grandfather committed suicide, after writing a note falsely claiming responsibility for Ryder's injuries.

In October of 2014, the true cause of the baby's fractures was finally discovered. The little guy suffered from Ehlers-Danlos syndrome (EDS). He, his mother, and his grandmother were diagnosed by Dr. Michael Holick at the Boston University Medical Center.

Maryland

Maryland Father Accused of Abuse over Broken Bones – Both Children Removed from Home of Loving Parents

Max and Justine Gibbs were blessed with their second child on February 15th, 2014 in Lexington Park, Maryland. When their daughter was 8 weeks old, Max noticed her leg was swollen. Since Justine is a nurse, they trusted the medical profession and believed that they would provide assistance to their daughter. Hospital test results showed 3 ribs and one femur were fractured in their daughter.

The questioning about abuse began and the Gibbs described the questioning as an interrogation. Maintaining his innocence, Max was arrested on 2 counts of child abuse and 2 counts of assault. Max had never been in trouble with the law, he was terrified and couldn't believe what was happening.

Max and Justine took matters into their own hands and started researching. Justine went through testing and was diagnosed with Ehlers-Danlos syndrome, hypermobility type. This type of EDS is classified as loose joints and chronic joint pain, a connective tissue disorder. Believing their daughter to also have EDS, the Gibbs requested that she see a geneticist.

The judge will not clear Max of all charges until the geneticist sees their daughter, and talks to the CPS abuse specialist. Although the doctor has contacted the abuse specialist, not just by phone several times but additionally by email, the abuse specialist has not returned any communication. The abuse specialist is now stating, according to the Gibbs family, that she does not have to abide by the court order and speak to the doctor. So their daughter still remains unseen by the geneticist, even though there is a court order in place, as CPS plans to adopt out both children.

Massachusetts

Will Massachusetts Doctor Send Another Innocent Parent to Prison Over Shaken Baby Syndrome Accusation?

A Massachusetts father faces up to 15 years in prison after being convicted of Shaken Baby Syndrome. Sentencing is set to occur on September 24. The testimony of child abuse specialist, Dr. Alice Newton, played a major role in his conviction. She is the same doctor who accused Justina Pelletier's parents of medical child abuse so that the state could medically kidnap Justina. Her testimony was behind 2 other cases of parents spending time in jail for Shaken Baby Syndrome - cases which were later overturned and dropped.

Another Medical Kidnapping at Boston Children's Hospital: Baby Seized Over Formula Disagreement

Unable to pump enough breast milk for her prematurely born baby, the search began for an appropriate formula to feed baby Bella. Finding one that worked, they took their baby home to Alabama.

A trip back to Massachusetts, their former resident state, to gather belongings and visit family members resulted in difficulties in finding the same formula they had used in Alabama. They found one that the baby tolerated, but a visit to the local WIC office in Massachusetts put them at odds with a pediatrician who insisted on changing her formula, to one that baby Bella did not do well with as her weight allegedly began to decline.

The parents decided to go back to Alabama immediately, to be with a pediatrician who was using the right formula. But Massachusetts DCF followed their case to Alabama, contacting Alabama DHR. Alabama DHR investigated the family, and cleared them after seeing how well the baby was doing.

But this was not good enough for Massachusetts DCF, which allegedly threatened the family with criminal charges if they did not return to Massachusetts. The frightened family complied, and their baby girl was put into Boston Children's Hospital, where they soon lost custody. Now, Massachusetts DCF is planning to adopt out baby Bella.

Michigan

10-Month Old Baby Medically Kidnapped in Michigan

Michigan parents Josh Soto and Alexandria Burgess took their ten-month-old baby girl Selena to the pediatrician on September 1, 2015 because she was fussy, tugging on her ears, cutting teeth, had severe diaper rash, and seemed to have pain in her legs.

The pediatrician didn't seem concerned, and gave her Benedryl and a cortisone cream for her diaper rash. He suggested that they keep an eye on her but didn't note any concerns.

Ten days later, on September 11, 2015, Selena's pain seemed to have increased so they took her to the E.R. of a local hospital, Promedica-Bixby in Adrian, MI. The attending nurse initially ordered a hip x-ray, but Alexandria and Josh requested that they x-ray her legs, too, to be thorough.

When the doctor came back into the room she said she had two broken legs, and asked "How did this happen?" They were referred to the University of Michigan Mott Children's Hospital in Ann Arbor where a child abuse doctor determined that Selena had been abused, and had Child Protection Services take custody of the child.

The mother states: "We did everything we were supposed to as parents, and yet still found ourselves in this nightmare. This time, these moments with her.....we never get it back. Her first birthday, Thanksgiving, Christmas, her first time saying 'Momma,' her first steps.....all away from home. All ruined by this nightmare we've been thrown into."

Once Thriving Michigan Teenager Now Facing Death in CPS Custody

A Michigan social worker asked the mother of a 14 year old girl if she has life insurance on her daughter, Abbie Odonnell, after the 5' 9" teen went from 145 lbs to 92 lbs under CPS custody. Her twin sister Alexis is being housed in a maximum security juvenile detention facility. Her bunkmate has reportedly murdered 7 people. Their 17 year old sister Alyssa is being held in another lockdown facility. The girls' crime? The twins admitted to smoking pot on one occasion. Later the twins ran away from an abusive foster home. For the heinous crime of escaping that abuse, CPS is forcing the twins to serve a 12 month sentence in Wolverine Secure Treatment Center, and forbidding their older sister, who has done nothing wrong, to go home.

Laura Dalton doesn't think that Abbie will survive that long. Apparently, her social worker doesn't either, but is not doing anything to fix the situation.

Laura says that it has already been 17 months, and the girls have learned their lesson. They shouldn't have been smoking marijuana. They know that now. But is that infraction worth the state of Michigan endangering the very lives of these once healthy, thriving kids?

Michigan Teen Medically Kidnapped and Placed in Juvenile Detention Facility as Her Health Deteriorates

Last year Leiani McMichael was an honor student, artist, and a varsity swimmer at her high school. She was a good kid with a great life. Now the Michigan teenager's family fears for her life. The 17 year old was seized from her family by Child Protective Services on November 4, 2015, after the University of Michigan C. S. Mott Children's Hospital called CPS and accused her mother of Munchausen by proxy. The family and supporters believe that Mott is trying to cover up their poor care of Leiani. Doctors and social workers are blaming the teen for her debilitating illness, but her mother, Rebecca Campos-Santana, insists that there is no way this is all in her head - it's in her digestive system.

Currently Leiani is being held in Children's Village, a juvenile detention center. Jennifer Torres is the foster care placement specialist, and she has allegedly told the family that Leiani is at the juvenile detention center because there is currently no "safe place" to send her that can provide medical care. She has allegedly told the teen that she is never coming home, and that she cannot get out of the facility unless she gets out of the wheelchair, because the "good" foster families aren't wheelchair accessible.

Michigan Family Traumatized by CPS in Medical Kidnapping of Twins

"Let me tell you, there is nothing worse than being accused of abusing the kids that you would lay down your life for. I knew we never hurt our kids, as they are our whole reason for being, so what was wrong?

I would have these moments of complete devastation and outright panic in the reality of what was happening. I remember being in CVS one day and the reality of the State of Michigan wanting to terminate my parental rights hit me. I became paralyzed and sobbed uncontrollably thinking I was going to collapse and trying to figure out who I could call to come get me. This on top of the countless nights I cried myself to sleep in Tony's arms.

Everything we do is for them. How this could be happening to us was beyond my comprehension.

Was it really necessary to show up at my house with 3 police officers unannounced and traumatize my kids forever? How does a system set up to protect the children not take into consideration the fact that what they are doing potentially causes an irreversible emotional damage that nothing could repair?"

Parents Falsely Accused by CPS Fight to Get Reputation Back – Pay Forced Hospital Bills

The parents did nothing wrong, yet their lives were turned upside down. They were falsely accused of abuse when they took their baby girl to the doctor for an accidental injury. Later, they were compared to "dolphins caught in a net." A child abuse doctor at Helen DeVos Children's Hospital (HDVCH) in Grand Rapids, Michigan, actually thanked them for "taking a hard hit for the greater good" of catching abused and neglected children. They were innocent.

Missouri

5 Children Kidnapped from Family in Missouri When Baby with Low Vitamin D Found with Broken Bones

December 21st, 2014 Rebecca Wanosik was blessed with her 5th child. A beautiful baby girl was born in her home in Lebanon, Missouri. It was an uncomplicated home birth, and she was assisted by her midwife.

But soon their family was completely torn apart when CPS came in and took all 5 of their children away, after the baby was found with fractured bones. Being now listed as "child abusers," Rebecca would later learn that she had Ehlers-Danlos syndrome, with low vitamin D levels for both her and her baby.

The quiet house is hard to deal with. Rebecca talks about the memories she holds onto – the screams of excitement when she picked her children up from school, the snuggles and wet kisses, and all the joys and hardship of motherhood. She is now left with a broken heart.

Now as their visits are supervised in an unnatural setting, she talks about medical kidnapping.

"Many people think that medical kidnapping is made up and think it doesn't happen, the truth is that it is very real."

Rebecca wants people to know this has been a life-altering, traumatic experience. She wants people to know this is a long road that no parent should have to travel.

Eight year old Jaxon Taken By Hospital When Parents Ask For Second Opinion

A Missouri doctor recently told a little boy that, if she had it her way, he would never see his mommy and daddy again. This was after 8 year old Jaxon was seized from his parents' custody based solely on a statement from this single doctor. His parents, Tiffany and Jason Adams, are desperately trying to bring him home after what appears to be his doctor's retaliation because they "dared to seek a second opinion."

The Adams insisted that they had a right to seek another opinion. The doctor in charge of the care of their son replied: "I want you to know big hospitals take kids away from families for this stuff."

New York

Adult Medical Kidnapping in New York: 1950s Air Force Veteran Held Hostage in Hospital

Laredo Regular just wants to take his grandfather home, but a New York Hospital is keeping him hostage. Have we entered into a new age of "elder abuse" that includes medical kidnapping? Not happy with the medical treatment his grandfather was receiving, Laredo and his mom sought to transfer him to a different facility. They are the holder of a Health Proxy as well as POA (power of attorney) for their family member, and filled out the required forms for an AMA (Against Medical Advice) hospital discharge.

But the hospital would not discharge him, and later both Laredo and his mother were dragged out of the hospital room and banned from the hospital.

The Laredo family has sought help through various legal entities—the police, attorneys, and the political system. All of them, we are told, are in complete agreement with the family, but have not been able to get the hospital to budge from its decision to hold the grandfather against their will.

How can a hospital have so much power to defy police, attorneys, and the political system?

North Carolina

North Carolina Whistleblower Imprisoned, Daughter Kidnapped by CPS – Are Their Lives Now in Danger?

One Native American tribe's descent from a proud heritage into lawlessness and greed has gone unchecked for decades.

Until now.

In 2012, Randy Davis just wanted to obtain a box of his family's papers from his local tribal headquarters. Little did he know his questions would bring down retaliation that would include his daughter being kidnapped by CPS, theft, false imprisonment, uncounted civil rights violations, his name smeared, his livelihood lost, and his life forever changed.

Though the Croatan, as a people, still exist, many of its leaders appear to have sold out their birthright for state and federal largesse – not only changing their tribal name, but paying academics to eradicate the name from historical research and even illegally changing birth and death certificates.

In addition to this paper genocide being perpetrated against the tribe by its own, there is federal and state fraud and abuse, and lawless attempts to bribe, smear, coerce, kidnap and jail those members who might object or reveal the truth.

And then there is the "reservation shopping" by the national casino and gambling interests who have literally stolen the Croatan's historical records, apparently in an effort to "create" a tribe worthy of federal recognition, with the accompanying right to set up casinos, netting billions of dollars for those who control it.

One man stumbled into all of this unwittingly, setting off such retaliation that he has considered seeking witness protection for himself and his daughter.

Infant with Brittle Bones Medically Kidnapped in North Carolina as Mother is Arrested

When police arrested North Carolina mother Marty Peele on charges of child abuse last summer, her friends say they knew there had to be another explanation for 4 month old Micah's injuries. They say the picture painted by the media was inconsistent with what they know of Marty; and she couldn't possibly have done the things she has been accused of.

Petreana Anderson is one of Marty's friends. She considers herself "a pretty good judge of character." She told Health Impact News: "I hate that they [the media] painted her as a monster. That woman wouldn't hurt anybody."

Local media reported that Marty was accused of breaking 12 of Micah's ribs and 2 shoulder blades, as well as leaving deep bite marks. However, several expert doctors have now issued reports that there are indeed very plausible explanations for Micah's injuries, and they strongly assert that he was not abused.

Child Protective Services has ordered her not to have any contact with her baby, or with any other child under age 18, and she is facing a criminal trial for felony child abuse.

North Carolina Child Medically Kidnapped Starving to Death in Foster Care

A North Carolina grandmother is "horrified" at the condition of her 4 year old grandson Malakai. The deterioration in his health reportedly happened after Child Protective Services removed him from his family and placed him in foster care. She reports that he had previously been very healthy, with no medical problems. Now, the foster parents are collecting disability payments for him and he looks like he is starving. Kimberly Deese is fearful for her grandson's life.

The family claims that no matter what hoops they jump through or what evidence they provide, Wake County CPS seems determined to sever all family connection to Malakai Deese and adopt him out. Heather's parental rights have just been terminated, and CPS has made it clear that they refuse to consider placement of Malakai with his maternal grandmother, without basis, and in violation of both state and federal law. The family hopes to appeal, but they have only until December 4 to do so.

Ironically, the grandmother, Kimberly, had just finalized her adoption of another grandchild only a month before Malakai was seized by CPS - in the same county. Yet, when it came to Malakai, the social worker refused to do a home study or consider placing the toddler with his grandmother.

A Year After Emergency Room Visit, North Carolina Couple Still Fighting for Medically Kidnapped Newborn

In what is becoming an all-too-familiar scenario, a young couple living in Fayetteville, North Carolina, took their baby to the emergency room when he was not acting right, only to find themselves almost a year later still battling to bring their child home out of Child Protective Services' custody.

Ohio

Two Sisters of Homeschooling Family in Ohio Removed from Parents During Hospital Visit

Homeschooling mom Hildy Straightiff took her two daughters (ages 12 and 13) to a hospital in Ohio because their ketone levels had become too high. Both of her daughters suffer from Type 1 diabetes and are at risk for diabetic ketoacidosis, requiring them to watch their ketone levels.

While in the hospital, Child Protection Services in Clinton County had a judge remove custody of her two daughters, and she was not allowed back into the hospital. The girls' grandparents were allowed to stay in the hospital for a couple of days, but then the girls were separated and taken to different foster homes, to live in a place where they had never been before with people they had never met, while the grandparents and parents helplessly watched their lives take a dramatic turn.

Hildy Straightiff was told she had "mental health problems" and was not able to take care of her diabetic daughters.

In order for the father to receive permission to bring his daughters home, CPS ordered the mother, Hildy, to leave their home.

Hildy had a visit with her daughters on August 3, 2015 and said that her oldest daughter, Taylor, was in tears when she said, "Mommy, I hope that someone will help so we can be together again."

Ohio CPS Destroys Family of 5 Children – Parents Acquitted of Any Wrong Doing

Chris and Kathy Butner of Ohio answered their door one day and found two policemen and Child Protection Services there to take away their 5 children. They asked "Why?" but no explanation was given. They were told that "everything was going to be just fine."

They reportedly complied with everything CPS told them to do, and CPS allegedly told the parents that reunification was the goal. But their children were apparently being told by their foster parents that they were going to be adopted. They were frightened, and their parents told them not to worry, as they would soon be home.

Originally accused of Munchausen by proxy, Kathy says the court later found no evidence of abuse or medical neglect. But apparently that did not matter. Their visits to their children were cut off, and the children were adopted.

Chris and Kathy have been told there is nothing that can be done for them now that they have been adopted, and that they should just move on.

They ask, "How? Could you just move on?"

Kathy still hears her oldest son saying, "I thought you made me a promise?" Those words don't go away for Kathy and her husband. There is no closure for them. Not a day goes by in that home that was once filled with their children's laughter where the silence continues to take over their minds. Their children have now been led to believe that they have stopped fighting. They want their children to know they have not stopped fighting, and they will not give up.

Oklahoma

Cleared of Criminal Charges, Yet Infant Taken Away from Family for Failure to Thrive

They kicked her out of the hospital and took her baby away from her over a month ago. She hasn't seen her since. They won't even tell her where her daughter is. Jamie Martin took her baby Hope to the hospital because she and the doctors were concerned about Hope not gaining weight, no matter what they tried. Instead of finding answers, she lost her baby and she is devastated. Now DHS of Oklahoma is trying to terminate Jamie's parental rights to her baby girl.

"I have done nothing wrong to my baby. She is my miracle child. I need my daughter back!"

Jamie Martin is the typical girl-next-door in America's heartland. She works as a substitute teacher in her local elementary school. She volunteers and is on the board of a tornado disaster relief organization.

Her 8 year old son was thrilled when he found out that he was going to be a big brother.

Yet now Jamie has found herself in the middle of every parent's worst nightmare - her baby has been taken away from her.

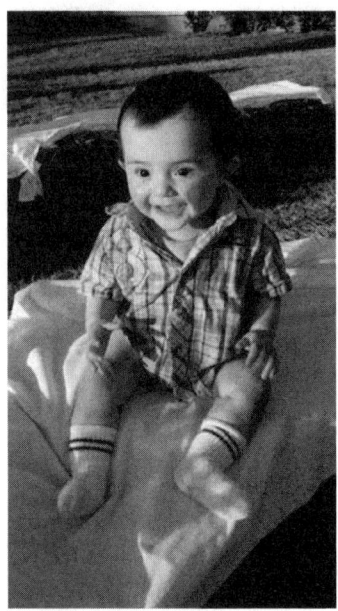

Oklahoma City Parents Lose Their 2 Children to CPS Due to "Shaken Baby" Allegation

An Oklahoma City couple has lost both of their children to CPS after taking their son to the hospital. He was injured while playing in a "bouncy chair," according to the parents. The father was accused of "abuse," and their parental rights were severed when a court appointed attorney allegedly did not put up much of a defense in their trial.

The parents have a new attorney now, and are appealing their case in the hopes that the children will not be adopted out of foster care. The parents have not seen their babies

Aleck and Mariposa since they were taken under state supervision on February 17, 2015.

Oklahoma Takes 3 Children Away from Parents When One is Found with Possible Brittle Bone Disease

April and Joshua Whinery report that they won't ever give up fighting for their children who were medically kidnapped by DHS in Oklahoma. According to Joshua, it started "all because I took my child to the hospital."

Degenerative bone disease runs in his family, yet the couple was accused of abuse. Though the family has repeatedly asked for him to be tested, DHS has allegedly refused to allow the test, attempting instead to terminate all of the couple's parental rights.

The last they heard, Hazel, who is almost 5 now, was praying every morning and night to be able to see her parents. It has been almost a year now since the Whinerys have been permitted to see their kids. All visits were cut off last March with Hazel, Travis, 3 1/2, and Aiden, who turned 2 in December. DHS reportedly told the family:

"You're never going to get your kids back, so it is best to cut it off now and get the kids in counseling."

Oregon

Ten Year-old Girl with Cystic Fibrosis Medically Kidnapped in Oregon

Mariah Mumpower is a ten year old little girl with cystic fibrosis (CF) who was taken away from her mother by Oregon Child Protective Services (CPS) in September 2015 during a routine visit to the CF clinic in Portland, Oregon.

The shelter order allegedly claimed that her mother, Rhonda Mumpower, was neglecting her child because she was underweight.

The seizure of her daughter also occurred shortly after she complained about the services at Doernbecher Children's Hospital CF clinic in Portland, and stated that she wanted to find a different clinic to take her daughter to for medical services.

Mariah was also asked to participate in a Harvard University backed research study on her rare form of cystic fibrosis.

Mother Loses 3 Children Because "Daughter is Too Short"

It's true - Angela Borths' daughter is short. So is she - just under 5 feet tall. In fact, being short runs in the family. But that didn't stop her pediatrician from allegedly reporting her to Child Protection Services (CPS). The petite mother has now had her 3 youngest children taken by the state of Oregon on grounds of "medical neglect," because her 6 year old daughter is short, and because she says she missed an appointment for her son when there was a 2 month lapse in their Obamacare insurance.

"I shouldn't have to defend my family for being short."

Pennsylvania

Medical Kidnapping in Pennsylvania: Parents of Baby with Rickets Accused of Abuse

Pennsylvania mother Jessica Battiato is frustrated with a doctor and a system that refuses to look for the medical cause of her baby's condition, instead placing the blame on the parents. Since her son Cesar, now 5 months old, was taken by child protective services 2 months ago, he has been diagnosed with rickets and hypotonia by a radiology expert. However, CPS seized custody of Cesar in April, based on accusations by Penn State child abuse specialist, Dr. Kathryn Crowell, that Cesar's injuries could only be caused by abuse.

Dr. Crowell has been accused of falsely testifying against parents before. In a 2009 case she accused a parent of child abuse which led to a father spending over a year in jail. A jury later found him not guilty.

Jessica wants answers for her baby, and she wants her baby back home, not in a foster home.

"My son needs medical attention. He doesn't need to be neglected by the state."

South Carolina

South Carolina Family has Children Medically Kidnapped Based on Wrong Diagnosis from Child Abuse Specialist

When Tai Simmons-Roper and her husband Shawn took their 4 week old baby Braxton to Greenville Memorial Hospital in South Carolina for excessive spitting up, the last thing they expected was that doctors would find multiple unexplained fractures, and that they would be thrown into jail and have their beloved new baby taken away from them by Child Protective Services. They were facing the possibility of spending the next 35 years in prison. They had no way of knowing that their son had serious metabolic bone disease, nor did the Child Abuse Specialist who reported them test Braxton to rule out such conditions before reporting them for child abuse.

After later medical reports were sent to the DA confirming that Braxton actually has infantile rickets and Ehlers-Danlos syndrome, all criminal charges were dropped. However, DSS (Department of Social Services) is still refusing to give custody back to his parents. Braxton's older brother was also taken away, and DSS will not let him go home either.

Another Baby Medically Kidnapped in South Carolina over Broken Bones – Parents Thrown in Jail

Jason and Mattie Walls from South Carolina took their frail, premature daughter to the emergency room after she became limp and was not breathing properly. What followed next was a chain of events resulting in every parents' worst nightmare: the seizure of their daughter, her removal from their custody, and charges made against them for child abuse which resulted in spending time in jail - all because they took their baby to the hospital looking for help.

Four Boys in South Carolina Medically Kidnapped When Parents Ask for Second Opinion

A parent's worst nightmare happened on July 10, 2015 in Spartanburg, South Carolina for the Headley family. The Spartanburg County Police walked right in the front door of the Headley's home while Danielle and her four boys were sleeping. William Headley had left for work earlier that morning and the front door was unlocked because the family felt safe in their community.

Danielle stated that a female officer, later identified as Investigator Tracy Moss, walked into her bedroom and asked if she was Danielle Headley. Danielle replied that she was. Danielle states:

"The cops busted into my house, didn't knock or identify themselves. She (the investigator) said they have a search warrant and you need to get up and get up now!"

Investigator Moss proceeded to demand that Danielle remove Jack from the crib in her room, unhook his feeding tube and bring him into the family's living room.

When Danielle walked into the living room, her three older boys were lined up on the couch. Danielle stated that:

"Apparently she got my kids from their bedrooms before she came into my room."

According to Danielle, there were five or six officers to assist executing a search warrant for all electronics and medications in their home. The Emergency Removal Order served on that day states that they were contacted by Greenville Health System, Dr. Nancy Henderson, and the Headley's four children needed to be removed due to the mother being suspected of Munchausen syndrome by proxy.

Danielle had made the mistake of asking for a referral to another hospital for their youngest boy, who has had health problems since he was born. Now, all four of her boys have been kidnapped by the State. And they are threatening to vaccinate the youngest boy against the parents wishes, even though he is known to have severe reactions to vaccines.

South Dakota

Healthy 17 Year Old Dies Shortly After South Dakota Takes Custody Away from Mother

A 17 year old boy is dead, and his mother wants answers. The answers that Dawn Van Ballegooyen has been given by the state of South Dakota don't make sense to her, and her mother's intuition tells her that somebody is covering up what really happened to her son, Brady Alan Folkens, while he was in state custody.

Most of the stories that we cover at Medical Kidnap have to do with children who were taken by the state via Child Protective Services, but there are other avenues for the state to acquire custody of minors, especially teenagers. As this heartbreaking story shows, the results can be just as devastating, no matter which government agency decides that it can do a better job of raising a child than the parents.

Just as with CPS cases, Dawn was not given a choice in her son being taken from her.

After failing a drug urine test at school, and being accused of belonging to a gang simply because he wore his hat backwards at school, a healthy 17 year old, Brady Folkens, was sent away to an "Academy Boot Camp" far away from his home. He could only talk to his mother 10 minutes a week on the phone.

Two months later, when his mother made a Christmas trip to visit him, she found him dead in the hospital.

Parents Find Injury to Baby After Daycare, Doctor Visit Results in CPS Removing all 3 Children

A South Dakota couple still can't figure it out. All they know is their three children, all under 3 years old, have been taken away for reasons they cannot fully explain because it makes no sense to them. They also have no idea how to get their children back from Child Protective Services (CPS).

They did what any other parent would do, and for that, Molly Bowling and Michael Becker report they had their children taken away from them.

Tennessee

Baby Found with Broken Bones – Parents Assumed Guilty of Abuse and Lose Custody

Keshia Turner understands why authorities wanted an investigation. She and her husband Chris want answers, too. They desperately want to know what is wrong with their baby boy, Brayden, because something is clearly wrong. She believed that the investigation would lead to a medical explanation being found for her baby's medical and developmental issues, an explanation that would demonstrate that they are loving, dedicated parents, and would lead to proper treatment for their child.

However, a Child Abuse doctor at Vanderbilt Children's Hospital accused Keshia of abuse instead. With no formal charges filed, and no trial or hearing conducted for over 9 months now, Keisha and her husband have lost custody of their baby who is no longer breastfed. And they can only visit him 1 hour per week.

Accusation of Shaken Baby Syndrome in Tennessee Destroys Family – Lands Parents in Jail

On August 15, 2013, in Jonesborough, Tennessee, Joe Whitaker frantically spoke to 911 as he tried to save his seven month old son, Jaden. According to Joe, the ambulance raced into their driveway; a female Emergency Medical Technician (EMT) jumped out, grabbed Jaden from his arms, slammed the ambulance doors, and sped away. Joe stood in the driveway watching the ambulance pull away, confused with the events that just occurred. What happened? Where were they taking his son? Why did they leave without him?

Seconds later, Charlotte Whitaker reached her house and saw Joe standing in the driveway. Her heart jumped into her throat. Where was her son? Luckily, the second rescue truck was still in front of her house, and the driver told the terrified parents that their son was being taken to Johnson City Medical Center (JCMC) in Johnson City, Tennessee. Why would the ambulance leave the parents in the driveway?

According to Charlotte, this is one of many incidences that would be twisted by CPS to aid them in falsely accusing the Whitakers of child abuse and taking their baby. This question became "Why didn't Joe Whitaker get into the ambulance with his son?" rather than "Why did the rescue personnel leave the parents behind?"

Later that day their other two children would be taken away from their school, never to return home again, while both parents would later be arrested and accused of "Shaken Baby Syndrome."

Texas

Houston Couple Gagged and Told to Fire CPS-fighting Attorney in Order to See Medically-Kidnapped Child

Earlier this year, in May of 2015, we reported on the story of the Giwa family in Houston, who had their 19-month old son medically kidnapped by Texas CPS. Randy Wallace of Fox News Houston broke the story.

Ahmed Giwa, the father of 19-month old Ali, contacted Health Impact News and MedicalKidnap.com at that time about publishing their full story. This was the last statement we received from him by email in May 2015: "Currently waiting for the Police outside the hospital where they have our son because CPS said they should not allow us in. Let us schedule next week outside Monday please. The Police (are) here now."

Multiple attempts to contact Ahmed to follow up after this email was received were unsuccessful. We suspected that a gag order had been placed on the parents in an attempt to stop the media and the public from learning any more about their story.

Both Ahmed and his wife Olubunmi have now contacted Health Impact News; and they want the world to know their story. Not only were they issued a gag order and told not to talk to the media, they were told they had to fire their attorney if they wanted to see their son again. The family had retained the services of Attorney Julie Ketterman in Houston, who has a history of fighting back against CPS and standing up for family rights. She has publicly stated: "CPS profits every time they place a child outside the home for adoption. It has stopped being a resource for families in need and has instead turned into an adoption mill."

Will the people of Houston and Texas continue to allow these gross abuses of Constitutional rights to continue in their state?

CPS Kidnaps 11 Children from Texas Homeschooling Family

Claire Rembis was sick, and had to spend 3 days in the hospital. Her attack of pancreatitis paled in comparison to what happened next. The mom from Plano, Texas, came home to a nightmare that no parent should ever have to face. CPS came and took her children, all 11 of them, because a "well-meaning" couple, members of her oldest son's former youth group, didn't think that the 16 and 14 year olds could handle babysitting their siblings while their dad took the baby to the hospital to visit Claire. The 16 year old made a dramatic escape and eluded CPS for days, until a judge allegedly determined that the seizure and removal of the children was illegal, and allowed them to return home.

Has it really gotten to the point where a mother cannot get sick without risking losing her children to the state?

The traumatized family's problems are not over, unfortunately. They must vacate the house where they are currently living by August 8, and CPS is continuing to harass the family by allegedly attacking their homeschooling program and requiring the mother to stop breastfeeding their 3 month old baby. They show up at their home unannounced whenever they please, and the family fears that the children could be kidnapped back into state custody at any time.

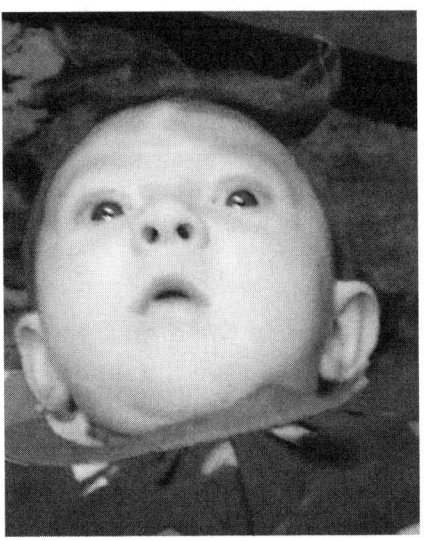

4 Month Old Texas Baby Seized from Parents in Medical Dispute

The Texas mother of a four-month old baby girl writes, "I just want her back home in my arms and love and kiss on her! To hold her and never let go!" But it has been a month now since little Kathryn Blalock was literally taken out of her mother's arms by CPS and the UMC Children's Hospital in Lubbock, Texas, in what appears to be another medical kidnapping.

Lorie, the mother of Kathryn, feels as though she is living a nightmare, amidst contradictory information and diagnoses from the doctors. Despite doing everything she could to follow all of the doctors' instructions, her baby was abruptly removed from her custody and is now in medical foster care away from the family who loves her.

Vermont

Vermont Teen Drugged Against Her Will, Held in Custody in Massachusetts Mental Health Facility

"I'm just literally here as a hostage. I didn't do anything. I haven't harmed anyone. I haven't harmed myself, and they won't let me go home. I just want to go home to my mom, so I can have my life back. They took it from me. They are drugging me up every single day against my will."

This is the heartfelt plea recorded by a homeschooled American teenager being held in a mental health facility in Massachusetts against her will and that of her family in Vermont.

Virginia

Devastated Parents of Children Medically Kidnapped in Virginia Fight Back

In a nightmare story that has become all too familiar to those of us at Health Impact News, parents in Virginia reached out to us to expose a corrupt system that has ravaged families all across America, and is completely out of control. Trying to find solutions to medical problems for their family, these parents did what families all across the United States do every day: they took their children to see medical doctors. Not finding solutions to their family illness, these parents pressed on to find answers. The result was that they were allegedly accused of having a mental disorder, Munchausen Syndrome by Proxy, and even denied medical care. Worse, their children were terrorized and kidnapped out of the hospital by force.

"My daughter ran screaming and crying to an old folks' home next to the hospital, locked herself in the bathroom, and called me. When I got there from our house down the street from hospital, my son was inside of a van with no handles on the inside and my daughter was in the bathroom surrounded by six to eight police. One cop from Shenandoah County looked at my fourteen year old son and saw tears in his eyes and asked in a mean way, 'What is wrong with you, why are you crying?!?' It was awful."

Lane and Susan have their children back now, but they want the world to know their story. They feel their children have been scarred for life: "My daughter is now back with me and is no longer a child, she left me believing in fairies and Santa and came back waking screaming every night, scared to death of being taken."

This family has lost their home, their jobs, and their health, but they are not done. They are fighting back, and currently have a lawsuit pending in federal court.

Washington

From Bubby's Best Birthday to Parent's Worst Nightmare: Medical Kidnapping in Washington

Since last week, Brandi and Thomas Everson have been fighting to regain custody of their son Bubby in Washington State. CPS made allegations of medical abuse against the Eversons and removed their medically fragile child after he gained national media attention for a special birthday wish.

The Eversons have a court hearing at 1:30 p.m. today (June 1, 2015) in their fight to get their son back.

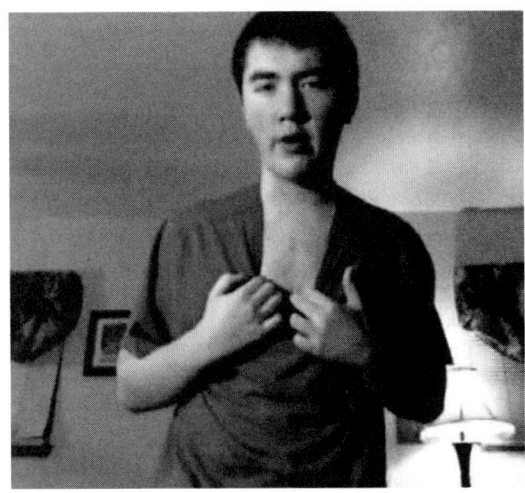

Was Medical Kidnap in Washington State a Cover-up for Medical Malpractice?

Being worried about Child Protection Services (CPS) taking her child was the last thing on the mind of Anne Giroux, a mother living in Washington State who was seeking medical treatment for her son, Kevin Kulman. Kevin started having concerning symptoms which drove her to take him to multiple doctor visits looking for an answer. She worried about having a family history of heart disease and why the doctor wasn't concerned nor would he give her a referral to a cardiologist. Instead Kevin was allegedly misdiagnosed as having asthma.

On May 21, 2012 Kevin suffered a heart attack while at school during his physical education class. The explanation of why he suffered the heart attack was a rare congenital heart condition which had been previously undetected. Not only did Kevin need open heart surgery, but later CPS took custody of Kevin claiming that Anne suffered from Munchausen syndrome by proxy.

Anne writes: "If a doctor performs an operation and prescribes drugs for my child based upon ME having Munchausen by proxy, what PSYCHIATRIC MALADY afflicts THE DOCTOR?"

Breastfed, Homebirthed Babies Taken Away From Parents For Not Using Hospital

All three of their babies have been taken away from them and placed in the care of strangers. Levi was 10 months old when his mother, local singer and songwriter Erica May Rengo, gave birth to his twin brother and sister, at their home in Bellingham, Washington.

"Our birth was glorious," she said, and the twins were reportedly healthy, full-term babies, who had no problem quickly figuring out how to breastfeed. The little family was overjoyed, until CPS stepped in to "help."

It is another medical kidnapping according to the parents. The Rengos have chosen a wholesome, holistic lifestyle, based in their Christian faith. But CPS has stepped in to allegedly override the parents' decisions. Now Erica and Cleave are living what they call a nightmare, separated from their children for reasons that don't make any sense at all to them.

1st Amendment Rights: Making the Public Aware of the Medical Kidnapping Issue

When we started a whole website dedicated just to telling the family stories of medical kidnappings, and publishing investigative reports showing how this could possibly be happening within the United States, we encountered much opposition.

We have been threatened with lawsuits, we have endured denial of service attacks against our servers, and received many threatening emails.

But as long as the 1st Amendment of the U.S. Constitution remains in place allowing us the freedom to legally publish this information, we have no intention of backing down.

The rest of this book will explain why medical kidnapping and state-sponsored kidnapping is a real issue in the United States, putting every family in danger. This is a fact that cannot be disputed.

Child Trafficking in the United States: A Huge Business

Massive federal funding available to all states is provided by law today under the guise of "child protection."

From the 1974 Child Abuse Prevention and Treatment Act (CAPTA) to the 1997 Adoption and Safe Families Act (ASFA) signed into law by President Bill Clinton (handed to him by a Republican-controlled House and Senate), tens of BILLIONS of dollars of federal funding are available for "Child Protection."

The only thing the state needs to access this funding is: CHILDREN. If each state does not take children away from their families and put them into foster care and make them available for adoption as a ward of the state, they cannot avail of those funds.

Hundreds of thousands of government employees derive their jobs from this business, from social workers to judges sitting on benches in family and juvenile courts.

Therefore, this is a system resistant to reform – one that will fight hard to keep the status quo. The fact that this system is plagued by corruption and that children more often than not are harmed by the system rather than helped, is not even in dispute anymore.

Some may object to my use of the term "child trafficking;" but the fact that children are trafficked in the United States is openly admitted. Even our own U.S. government admits that this is happening.

Sen. Rob Portman (R-Ohio) published a six-month investigation[1] in February of 2016 looking at 125,000 unaccompanied minors who have crossed the U.S. borders into the United States. This U.S. Senate report concluded that the Office of Refugee Resettlement, an agency of the Department of Health and Human Services (HHS), has failed to protect these children from human trafficking, leaving them vulnerable to abuses at the hands of government-funded social service agencies.

The fact that the United States is a popular destination for child trafficking has been well documented:

"The causes of the surge of UACs are disputed, but all stakeholders, including HHS, agree that one reason UACs come to this country is that they are 'brought into the United States by human trafficking rings.' According to the State Department's 2015 Trafficking in Persons Report, '[t]he United States is a source, transit, and destination country for men, women, transgender individuals, and children—both U.S. citizens and foreign nationals— subjected to sex trafficking and forced labor.' Human trafficking involves transporting or harboring human beings, often for financial gain, through the use of fraud, force, or coercion."[1]

As we will show you in the pages to follow, however, this problem of child trafficking is not limited to only alien children coming across our borders. It is a threat to every child in America today, as children are needed by the state to continue this multi-billion dollar child trafficking business.

Chapter 2: Medical Kidnapping in the U.S. – Kidnapping Children for Drug Trials

War Crimes Tribunal at Nuremberg. Adolf Hitler's personal physician, 43-year old Karl Brandt. Brandt was also Reich Commissar for Health and Sanitation, and was indicted by the U.S. prosecution with 22 other Nazi doctors. Brandt was found guilty of participating in and consenting to using concentration camp inmates as guinea pigs in horrible medical experiments, supposedly for the benefit of the armed forces. He was sentenced to death by hanging.

The U.S. federal government has mandated drug research with children. The need for children to participate in drug company research is high, and the temptation to overstep parental rights to force children to participate is great. Researchers publicly admit using money and other rewards to obtain participation of children in their drug trials.

Organizations that advocate for the rights of parents to make decisions regarding their children's healthcare are finding that foster children in CPS custody are being enrolled in drug experiments without parental approval. State Child Protective Services are enrolling children in drug experiments without parental approval or court orders. However, those who conduct these drug experiments for pharmaceutical companies, and those who are charged with monitoring such research, do not see a problem with their recruitment methods.

There is a Shortage of Children for Drug Research Studies

Kayla and Hannah Diegel suffer from a rare form of mitochondrial disease. They were removed from the custody of their parents in 2014 allegedly because the parents disagreed with their doctors. Are they subjects of a drug trial?

In a 2011 article in the Journal *Pediatrics*, researchers discussed the problem of recruiting children for participation in clinical trials for drug testing. Researchers from Ohio State University (Columbus) and Case Western Reserve University, confirm that the U.S. federal government is mandating that children be included in clinical research studies.

Dr. Tishler, PhD, and Dr. Staats Reiss, PhD stated:

"Since 1994, federal guidelines have called for the inclusion of children in clinical studies. Related federal incentives and laws such as the "pediatric rule" (the Pediatric Research Equity Act) and the pediatric exclusivity provision have also been passed to increase the number of pediatric clinical trials launched by pharmaceutical companies. Despite these mandates, the allocations to pediatric clinical trials in federal and private research and development budgets have remained limited. In addition, pediatric researchers continue to experience difficulty locating children and families who are willing to enroll in clinical trials.

Recruitment for pediatric studies is hampered by several factors including ethical concerns with using children as subjects, regulatory oversight that is significantly more restrictive for child trials than for adult trials, a lack of research infrastructure, the need to obtain consent from parents, and the challenge of determining appropriate payments for participation that are not coercive."[1]

These researchers were struggling with ethical considerations concerning the use of money to entice parents to enroll their children in research studies. These researchers didn't think that parents should see the enrollment of their children in drug experiments as a money-making proposition. On the other hand, they realized that money and gifts were very useful for bringing more children into pharmaceutical drug research.

They also noted that the number of pediatric research participants has been increasing. In 2006, they found that there were approximately 45,000 children participating in experiments. There has also been an increase in the number of Phase I studies with normal healthy children. In their review, only 9,817 of the 39,628 studies listed on ClinicalTrials.gov included children.

The researchers indicated that one of the most pressing challenges in doing pediatric clinical research is the limited number of participants. Researchers often must network across sites or countries to gain adequate numbers of participants. They often must expend significant energy and resources locating potential subjects.

Dr. Tishler, and Dr. Staats Reiss discussed how money is often given in exchange for voluntary participation. They stated:

"One review of the Centerwatch.com clinical trials listing service published in 2002 revealed that nearly 25% of pediatric trials offered payments to participants that ranged from $25 for an investigation of influenza medications to $1500 for a psoriasis-medication study. In another study, [researchers] sent surveys to the IRB chairs [institutional review boards] at member institutions of the National Association of Children's Hospitals and the Office for Protection From Research Risks.

Sixty-six percent of these institutions used paid participants, and there was wide variation in payment practices across the sites (ranging from $1 to $1000 in cash and $500 in savings bonds). Many of the institutions in the Weise et al study (42%) used a combination of incentives and/or payments for both the children and parents."[2]

CPS Violates Parental Consent and Freedom of Speech

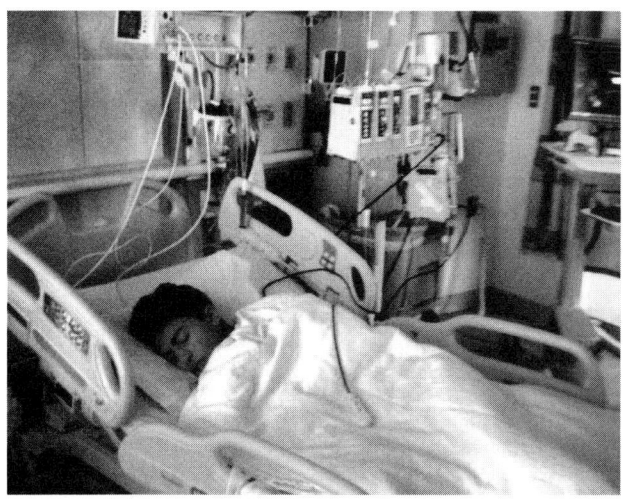

Isaiah Rider suffers from a rare condition called neurofibromatosis. When his mother took him to a hospital in Chicago that specializes in his condition, they ended up taking custody of him over the objections of his mother. Is Isaiah part of a drug trial?

There are two factors that normally limit child participation in medical and drug company research. The first is the requirement for parental consent. Children normally cannot participate unless a parent gives written consent. The second is the normal right that people have to publicly speak out in situations where parents and their children are being coerced and compelled to participate in drug company experiments.

We would expect that these two constraining factors would keep children safe from becoming unwilling participants in drug research. However, there are situations in which state agencies are able to avoid both of these constraints and force children to become human guinea pigs.

The network of state operated child protective service agencies (CPS) routinely circumvent the rights of parents and children, and give permission for physicians/researchers to force children to participate in drug company experiments.

Children who are in the foster care system and who are under the control of Child Protective Services are easily targeted for involuntary inclusion in drug experimentation. Ideally, even if children are under CPS control, their natural parents should retain the right to give consent for medical treatment for their children whether it is routine or experimental.

In practice, however, once CPS steps into a family's private life and takes children out of the home and places them in foster care, then parental oversight regarding the healthcare of their children is routinely violated. Because these cases are involved in State Juvenile or Family Courts (as opposed to Civil Courts), records are sealed and kept secret, supposedly to protect the children.

CPS Collects Federal Funds for Trafficking Children

Tonya Brown with adopted son Christopher, who had a rare form of Leukemia. Doctors and CPS took Christopher away when she disagreed with the doctors over his treatment.

There is money to be made and lots of it! Whenever a child enters state CPS control, federal funding flows into that state. It is in the best interest of state budgets to bring children into the CPS system and to keep them there as long as possible. States have a large incentive to take children and sever parental rights and put children up for adoption. Adoption brings even greater money into state budgets. The flow of money into CPS budgets helps maintain the jobs of CPS workers.

The Alliance for Human Research Protection testified to the U.S. Congress about the flow of money into state budgets. They reported:

"In 2004, the Federal Government provided more than $7 billion in dedicated funds for child protection. The bulk of these funds (almost $5 billion) supported children who had been removed from their homes."[3,4]

In 2007 Joseph Doyle, an economics professor at MIT's Sloan School of Management, published a study which tracked at least 15,000 kids in foster care from 1990 to 2002. It was the largest study of its kind at that time. *"Although foster care is meant to be a temporary arrangement, children stay in care for an average of two years, and there are currently over 500,000 children in care (US Department of Health and Human Services 2005). Roughly 60 percent of foster children return home; 15 percent are adopted; and the remainder "age out" of foster care (Fred C. Wulczyn, Kristen Brunner Hislop, and Robert M. Goerge 2000). Three quarters of these children live with substitute families, one-third of which are headed by relatives of the children. These families are paid a subsidy of approximately $400 per month per child (Child Welfare League of America 1999), and states spend over $20 billion each year to administer these child protective services (Roseana Bess et al. 2002)."*[5]

CPS and Medical Kidnapping

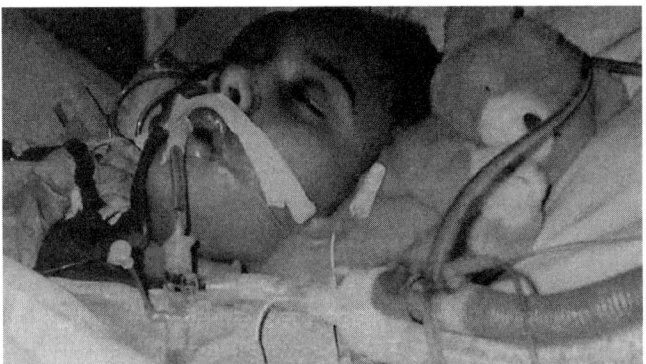

Chaunell Smith was taken away from her family by CPS after her mother questioned her treatment. Was her custody battle an attempt to cover up medical malpractice?

CPS takes control over all aspects of the lives of children. CPS severs contact between parents and their children when parents don't do what CPS demands, and will give permission for foster children to participate in drug experiments. This is done even when the drug trials may be life-threatening. This is done, so it is said, to protect the children, but such "protection" destroys the family unit, traumatizes children, and frequently results in permanent harm to children.

The process that results in CPS seizing children and placing them in foster care begins with allegations of parental neglect or harm against their children. It is not unusual to find that such allegations are without truth. Even so, CPS and the family court system may refuse to return children to their parents. Sometimes, after many months or even years, children are returned after the experimentation is complete. But in many other situations, children are simply put out for adoption. In these cases, unproven allegations against parents can result in permanent loss of children without any opportunity for future contact.[6]

Parents, who have done nothing wrong, find themselves without their children, and they have no recourse to get them back once they are adopted by others.

CPS Does Not Help Families, But Destroys Them

The lofty goal that CPS once had many decades ago to strengthen dysfunctional families and restore children to a safe and loving environment with their biological parents or with close relatives is long gone. Today, CPS does not fix families, rather, it destroys families in order to provide pediatric subjects for clinical drug trials, to provide desirable children for adoption, and to keep federal dollars flowing into the state CPS budget.

Children are even more likely to be kidnapped by CPS workers for medical experiments when they have rare diseases. Such children are highly prized subjects for experimentation. This happened in a nationally publicized case that was exposed in 2013. Justina Pelletier was abducted by officials at Boston Children's Hospital and subjected to disabling drug therapies.

As a result, 32 members of the U.S. House of Representatives cosponsored legislation in 2014, which was entitled "Justina's Law." The proposed legislation was intended to End Experimental Medical Research on Children Seized by CPS. Unfortunately, the proposed law never even made it out of the House subcommittee. The proposed law languished and died without action by Congress.

Congresswoman Spoke Out Against CPS Abuses Before her Murder

Georgia Senator Nancy Schaefer. Crusader against CPS before her murder.

Justina Pelletier was not an isolated example of CPS abuse. Similar abductions and medical experimentation have been taking place throughout the United States since the late 1980s.

The late state senator from Georgia, Nancy Schaefer, most likely gave her life in exchange for bringing CPS sponsored medical abuse to light.[7] She publicly exposed many cases of medical kidnapping, which involved CPS workers in numerous states.

Schaefer lost her Senate seat in Georgia as a result of speaking out, but stated it was something "worth losing" for standing up for the rights of parents who were having their children kidnapped by CPS. She and her husband were found murdered in their home in 2010. You can read her report on CPS in Chapter 6.

Nancy Schaefer describes the attack that is being waged against children for the purposes of drug experimentation and adoption. She points out how such state sponsored child abuse is ultimately an attack on the sovereignty of parents to make decisions for their family without coercion and manipulation from state agencies and the family court system. Neither of these organizations is operating to protect the family structure. They are operating under a new ethic, which is to do what is "right" for the child – and to ignore what is best for the entire family.

Children are now seen as autonomous individuals whom the state must protect from parents. The relationship between parents and their children is no longer valued and protected. Rather, parents are seen as potential offenders who are considered guilty of any charges that are brought against them. The wide range of parenting styles which was once permitted in our society is no longer valued. CPS workers, Family Court judges, and the authority of the state are now determining what is normal, and any parent who disagrees with them is subject to retaliation against their family and parental authority. Everything is based on what the state thinks is "best for children."

It's Now All about "What is Best for the Child" – Not the Family

As reported by Steven R. Isham M.A., L.B.S.W, in an article published by Health Impact News and MedicalKidnap.com, children who are seized by CPS and placed into long term foster care do very poorly when compared to other children. Foster care is not usually a safe refuge for damaged children, which allows them to heal. Rather, foster care perpetuates the abusive and neglectful patterns in the lives of many children, which sets them up for long-term failure as adults.

Steven Isham reveals that former foster children rarely become productive citizens who are able to take care of themselves. He indicated that by age 25, 61 out of 100 former foster children will be unemployed, 24 out of 100 will be homeless, 64 out of 100 males will be incarcerated, 32 out of 100 females will be incarcerated, and only 3 out of 100 will have been able to complete a four year college degree.[8]

See also: **Foster Care Children are Worse Off than Children in Troubled Homes** –
http://medicalkidnap.com/2015/05/13/foster-care-children-are-worse-off-than-children-in-troubled-homes-the-child-trafficking-business/

U.S. House of Representatives Investigates Medical Trials of Foster Children

Phil Crane, right, meets with President George W. Bush and Representative Bill Thomas of Committee on Ways and Means.

In 2005, a hearing with the title "Protections for Foster Children Enrolled in Clinical Trials" was held by the U.S. House of Representatives. The Subcommittee on Human Resources of the Committee on Ways and Means, investigated whether adequate safeguards were in place to protect foster children from being forced to participate in drug studies.

The allegation that they were investigating involved clinical drug trials on AIDS drugs that were conducted during the period from the late 1980s through 2001. In part they were looking back at the past and asking if there were abuses. They were also wondering whether there were any inappropriate actions taking place in more recent years.

The testimony could easily be divided into two camps.

The first camp could be called the professional camp. It consisted of U.S. Health and Human Services administrators, pediatricians, public health researchers, and CPS administrators. The second camp could be called advocates for injured children. This second camp consisted of representatives from various children's advocacy groups, biological parents of foster children who were taken by CPS, and various other individuals who were concerned about exploitation and forced experimentation on children.

In short, the professional camp did not believe there was a problem. They believed the use of existing institutional review boards (IRBs), which reviewed all experiments involving human subjects, would prevent abuse of children in foster care. They also believed that other random reviews conducted by the federal government would keep researchers from behaving unethically.

On the other hand, the camp that was advocating for parental rights and the protection of foster children told a very different story. They described medical abuse. They described individual events, and systemic problems, and called for reform of the CPS system.

Members of the congress are very busy people. They do not schedule hearings on potentially controversial topics unless there is already sufficient evidence to warrant the investigation. Sometimes hearings are held to emphasize a problem to raise awareness in preparation for their action. In other situations, hearings are scheduled and witnesses are carefully selected to quiet a politically hot situation, which could bring embarrassment or lead to allegations of criminal wrongdoing.

The subcommittee invited certain witnesses to speak to them and to answer questions. All of the witnesses were from the professional camp of government administrators, physician researchers, and CPS administrative staff. Invited witnesses were all directly involved in regulating drug experiments or responsible for conducting those experiments. Advocates for parents and children were not invited to speak, but were permitted to submit written testimony.[9]

Congress Knows Children are being Abused in the CPS System

Wally Herger – U.S. House of Representatives from California's 2nd district. Chairman Subcommittee on Human Resources of the Committee on Ways and Means. In office January 3, 1987 – January 3, 2013.

When the Subcommittee on Human Resources of the Committee on Ways and Means, U.S. House of Representatives met to examine this problem, Chairman Wally Herger, Representative from California made this statement:

"Over the last 18 months, this Subcommittee has heard hearings about a number of issues affecting kids in the Federal, State child welfare programs, and this issue is like many of them: It has the potential for being explosive. The child welfare program in the richest, most powerful country in the world is, and has been, often an abysmal failure.

Now, we don't need proof of more of that. We can give you all kinds of examples of it. We know about kids losing their lives in the child welfare system. Practically every State legislature every year deals with one case or another, and everybody wrings their hands, and the problems go on. The kids are sometimes locked up and sometimes starved under the supervision of the agencies. **We know the children have been used without proper supervision for drug testing**."[11](emphasis added)

The first witness to testify before the House subcommittee was Dr. Donald Young, M.D., U.S. Department of Health and Human Services, Principal Deputy Assistant Secretary for Planning and Evaluation. He provided extensive testimony regarding governmental oversight. Dr. Young concluded his remarks by stating:

"We continue to address challenges posed by the threat of HIV/AIDS and are committed to basic and clinical research to strengthen the nation's ability to cope with this infectious disease. The protection of human subjects, including children, in clinical trials has been and will remain a top priority for HHS. HHS is firmly committed to the protection of the rights and welfare of every individual who participates in human research consistent with sound ethical standards and regulatory requirements."

Later in the hearing, Dr. Young was asked if any changes were needed in regard to foster children and their participation in drug experimentation. Dr. Young stated:

"We are not aware of any changes that we believe need to be made. If they are identified, we will be very happy to consider them and make a decision as how best to proceed. We share with you the concern about the adequate protection of foster children. At the same time, the opportunity to let them participate and get the advantage of clinical research, if that is theirs and their guardian's decision."

Advocates for Parental Rights Blow the Whistle on Drug Trial Abuses

The testimony provided by advocacy organizations, parents, and concerned professionals told a very different story. Most were not interested in discussing the past AIDS drug trials, but were narrowing in on what they saw as current abuses in 2005.

Their testimony exposed a pattern of foster care abuse that has continued to worsen over the past ten years. The abuse now has to do mostly with forced experimentation on foster children with psychiatric drugs, or the treatment of children with very rare diseases.

Important testimony was given by representatives of Ablechild.org. Sheila Matthews stated:

"I am the National Vice President and Co-founder of Ablechild.org, a non-profit national parent organization that works on educating the public on the issues of informed consent and the right to refuse psychiatric 'treatment.' Our organization is very concerned with the outcome of this hearing because we hear directly from parents victimized by the trafficking of their children into clinical drug trials while in state custody.

Ablechild has documented cases of children who have been placed on drugs, completely unaware that they are participating in a clinical drug trial, and without knowing that they have the right to 'opt out' of participating. The fact is, the State holds the responsibility of providing informed consent to parents and children, and lacks any procedure to protect and safeguard this right.

Our organization points out the problems that resulted from strategies designed to target and exploit these children. The Connecticut Advocate reported these resulting problems in its June 5th, 2001 article, 'Study Calls for Review of Psychiatric Drugs Prescribed to Kids.' Within this news story, the authors of a new study questioned why 396 children under 4 years old covered by Medicaid were prescribed psychiatric drugs. Some of these children were less than 1 year old.

A clear conflict of interests exists between the pharmaceutical industry and the experimentation occurring on children within state custody. This fact is clearly demonstrated by workshops sponsored by the pharmaceutical and biotechnology industries designed to optimize strategies for drug development and trials in children."

Gloria Wright, also from Ablechild.org, added these comments to the subcommittee in a separate letter:

"As a grandparent and a member and officer of Ablechild, a 501(C) 3 organization, I wish to bring to your attention our cry for the protection of human rights of foster children across America!

Our organization frequently hears from parents across the nation who implore us for assistance in the matter of the clinical trial/experimental drugging of their children while in state custody and in foster care. These children have been placed on clinical trial drugs without a legal advocate responsible for safeguarding their health, or their life. As minors these children are unable to opt out of these tests/experiments, the parents have been denied their right to dissent and there obviously are no procedures in place to safeguard the rights of the children."

Statement of Linn Asplund, a parent from Waterbury, Connecticut:

"Thank you for considering my testimony. When my son was 10 years old, he was attending Washington School in Waterbury, CT. He started having problems in the beginning of third grade, September 1999. He was being picked on and bullied by the other children. His grades started suffering and he too started having discipline

problems. This bullying was brought to the school's attention, but it still went on. The principal suggested a PPT. I agreed and at the first PPT I agreed to have him tested. I was then told he was "LD" (Learning Disabled), but it was not that bad.

Next they told me they wanted him to see a psychologist for a psychological evaluation, I agreed. I obtained a copy of the evaluation. My son told the doctor that he had no friends at school. He liked it better at home and would wake up repeatedly at night with thoughts of how to quit school. By this time Dr. Abramavich said my son was psychotic and needed to be medicated. I refused. The next thing I knew, DCF (Department of Children and Families) was at my door telling me the school said my son has special needs that need to be taken care of. I still refused the psychiatric drugs. I brought him to "child guidance" and was told that he was a normal child.

After several visits from DCF I still refused to drug my son. On March 16th 2000, I found court papers on my doorstep. In them my husband and I were charged with abuse and neglect and were informed that DCF was going to take our son from us. Later that day a social worker and police officer arrived and took him away.

*Two weeks later, DCF placed him in Waterbury Hospital where Dr. Edwards gave my son Haldol and Attavan–mind altering drugs not approved for use in children. A few days after this, Dr. Mennessen put him on 100 mg of Wellbutrin a day; also not FDA approved for use in children. When I asked Dr. Mennessen why he was giving my son this drug without my consent, his reply was "**we need a number of cases to get it FDA approved**." (emphasis added)*

Conclusion: CPS and Doctors are Kidnapping Children for Medical Research

It is hard to determine the exact number of clinical drug trials that are currently in process in the United States, or to determine how many children are in such trials. This problem was identified at the House of Representatives hearing in 2005, and it still remains a problem ten years later.

If data from Europe can be used as a yardstick to compare the involvement of children in clinical studies, then the scope of drug testing on children has increased dramatically since the 2011 data, which was presented at the beginning of this article.

The European Union Clinical Trials Register currently displays 25,527 clinical trials, of which 3,662 are clinical trials conducted with subjects less than 18 years old. [10]

The CPS system is setup in such a way that its activities with specific families are secret. They hide behind confidentiality laws to prevent public oversight. They threaten parents with permanent loss of their children if they speak publicly. The family court system adds its authority to demand that parents remain silent. All the while, family after family is threatened and broken. Children are brought into drug experimentation programs, and others are provided for the adoption business, which brings even more money into state coffers.

CPS intentionally does not place children with family members, because the children bring in greater income to the state when they are placed in foster care homes. CPS often acts quickly to put children up for adoption, because the cash payments that the state will receive are substantial. In short, the violation of parental rights is a money making proposition for state governments. The money perpetuates the CPS system, and allows abuse to happen in the name of "protecting" children.

Physicians are required by law to report to CPS any situation that looks like child abuse or medical neglect. This is a ticket for CPS to investigate, seize children, meet their quotas, and start bringing money into the state budget. Since American culture has been trained to idolize and even worship the judgment of physicians, then most parents have little power to fight both the judgments of CPS and the medical establishment. The Family Court system works hand in hand with CPS and physician recommendations, and gives little respect to the desires of parents.

Children with rare diseases, especially rare genetic diseases, are very vulnerable to CPS medical kidnapping and abuse. If parents don't agree with a doctor's treatment plan, then the doctors can notify CPS that the parents are neglecting their children by not doing what the doctor recommends. Once this happens, parents lose the right to make independent decisions for their children.

Once control over a child's life is taken by CPS and the medical care system, then parental rights are ignored. Parents are not usually contacted to obtain permission to allow their children to participate in drug trials. If they are contacted, and refuse to give permission, then they will be ignored and may have future contact with their children denied. The parent's health insurance companies can be billed for treatments/services that parents did not approve. Payments can even be made for drugs given to children that have not been approved for use in children by the USFDA.

In a letter written by Sharon Schuldt to the House committee that examined clinical drug testing on foster children, she gave us a serious warning. She wrote:

"There was horrific disregard for humanity that took place in World War II Germany, some of which started out being directed toward the weak and vulnerable, in orphanages and hospitals, but then was directed to millions who lost their lives in the concentration camps. A society does not just lose their regard for human life overnight. It is a step at

a time downward and soon that society slips further and faster downward. Many vowed, 'Never Again.' We in the U.S. cannot and should not be allowing access to our children for medical research. There is no argument that justifies it!"

Chapter 3: Are New Pediatric "Child Abuse Specialists" Causing an Increase in Medical Kidnappings?

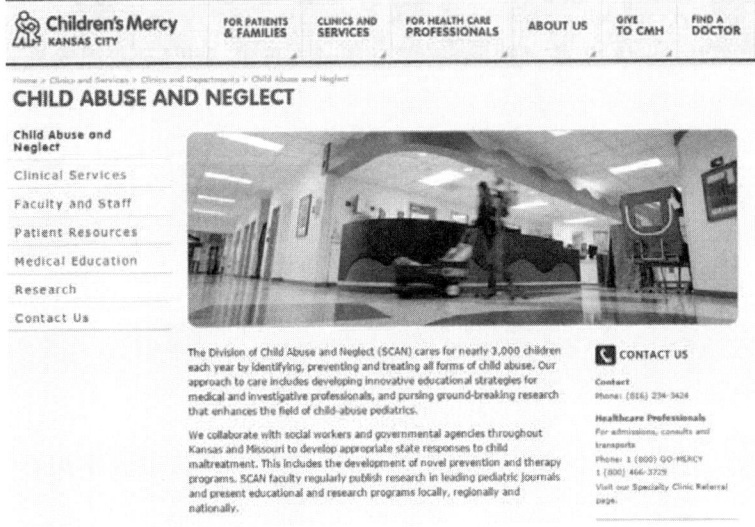

The Division of Child Abuse and Neglect (SCAN) clinic at Children's Mercy Hospital in Kansas City

What do the Salem witch trials of 1692 have in common with the experiences of Keshia and Chris Turner and their son Brayden, or Max and Justine Gibbs and their little baby girl? How do those events over 300 years ago illuminate what has happened recently to Jessica Battiato and her son Cesar, or Rebecca and Anthony Wanosik's little baby girl, or Brandon and Cynthia Ross and their son Ryder? Why does one of the most notorious events in American history seem to aptly apply to a new scientific subspecialty in pediatric medicine?

Two words: "witch hunt."

Keshia and Chris Turner and their son Brayden.

Keshia and Chris Turner from Tennessee sought medical help for their son Braden's medical and developmental issues. But instead, after a child abuse pediatrician at Vanderbilt Children's Hospital accused Keshia of abuse, the investigators and doctors allegedly stopped looking for any other explanation for Brayden's condition, and seized custody. He is now nine months old, and his mother says he cannot even sit up by himself, but doctors at Vanderbilt tell her that there is no need for any testing.

Jessica Battiato and her son Cesar.

Jessica Battiato from Pennsylvania has been blamed for child abuse by a doctor and a system that she says refuses to look for the medical cause of her baby's condition. Since her son Cesar, now five months old, was taken by Child Protective Services two months ago, her son has reportedly been diagnosed with rickets and hypotonia by a radiology expert. However, CPS took custody of Cesar, allegedly based on accusations by Penn State child abuse specialist, Dr. Kathryn Crowell, that Cesar's injuries could only be caused by abuse.

Maryland father Max Gibbs with daughter

Similarly, **Max and Justine Gibbs** from Maryland found their lives turned upside down after taking their 8-week old daughter to the hospital to check out a bruise. Max, a pastor with no previous troubles with the law, was arrested and put in jail on suspicions of abuse. He is now completely cut-off from BOTH of his children.

5 Children Kidnapped from Family in Missouri When Baby with Low Vitamin D Found with Broken Bones

In yet another sad story reported on MedicalKidnap.com, **Rebecca and Anthony Wanosik** from Missouri had all 5 of their children removed from their home after Rebecca brought their 3-week old daughter to the doctor to check on a condition with her ribs, while her husband was on active military duty.

Ross Family

Brandon and Cynthia Ross from Maine had their son Ryder taken away after bringing him to the hospital because his leg was swollen. Brandon, the father, was later arrested on charges of child abuse, and Cynthia's grandfather (the great-grandfather of the baby) became so upset that he committed suicide.

These are not isolated cases, but representative of what thousands of families around the U.S. are reporting is happening to them after taking their children to a doctor or hospital to check on broken bones, bruises, or other medical conditions.

A witch hunt is defined as "*seeking and persecuting any perceived enemy, particularly when the search is conducted using extreme measures and with little regard to actual guilt or innocence."*

For many traumatized children and families, this defines their experiences with children's hospitals and child abuse pediatricians, who seem intent on reaching a verdict, rather than evaluating all of the evidence.

New Pediatric Subspecialty: the "Child Abuse Pediatrician"

Child Abuse Specialist Kathryn Rausch Crowell, M.D. – Penn State Hershey Medical Group.

The rise in aggressive uses of CPS by doctors and hospitals diagnosing "child abuse," extensively documented by MedicalKidnap.com, appears to parallel several new developments in the world of pediatric medicine. In 2010, the American Academy of Pediatrics certified a new subspecialty in *child abuse pediatrics*, which requires a fellowship with a teaching hospital's child protection unit and a separate board exam.

The majority of the nation's 324 Child Abuse Pediatricians are housed within children's hospitals.

Children's Hospitals Build Entire Teams focused on Child Abuse

James Anderst, MD, MSCI, Section Chief of the SCAN Clinic, co-developed an animated program that is helping law enforcement, social workers and court officials work more effectively with medical professionals in determining whether injuries to children are accidental or the result of abuse. Terra Frazier, DO, a member of the SCAN Clinic staff, is helping deliver the program to interested organizations.

Image from childrensmercy.org.

Another related change is the focus by the National Association of Children's Hospitals and Related Institutions (NACHRI) to emphasize and define the role of child abuse teams at children's hospitals.

In 2006, the NACHRI provided a framework to aid understanding of the range of services offered, periodically updating, making benchmarks available and defining best practices. Thus, the child abuse specialists "frequently lead child protection teams that also include social workers, case managers and other clinical providers. These teams serve as a resource to children, families and communities by accurately diagnosing and treating abuse (as well as ruling out abuse); consulting with local child welfare agencies and law enforcement; testifying as experts in court; and directing child abuse and neglect prevention programs."[1]

The 2012 *Survey Findings of Child Abuse Services at Children's Hospitals* reports that:

"Children's Advocacy Centers (CAC) represent a well-known model through which many communities respond to suspected child abuse. A quarter of hospitals (33 out of 131) house a CAC. 62% (80 of 130) provide medical services to one or more independent CACs. 38 respondents neither house nor provide services to a CAC."

Child Abuse is Not A Medical Diagnosis, but a Legal Accusation

Dr. Deborah Lowen is a Child Abuse Specialist, and the head of the Child Abuse team at Vanderbilt. Image from vanderbilt.edu.

Essentially, these new child abuse pediatricians and their accompanying teams at children's hospitals are NOT specialists in orthopedics, neurology, psychology or numerous other subspecialties, but focus exclusively on determining a LEGAL allegation for a set of medical issues.

"Child abuse" is not a medical diagnosis, but due to its horrific nature, the allegation often seems to trigger a "witch hunt," sometimes ripping a sick child out of his or her loving family to languish, undiagnosed and untreated. Though abusive parents exist, and children's injuries can sometimes provide evidence of abuse, it is being frequently reported that more and more often a rush to judgment by doctors and CPS is destroying healthy families, and often damaging the very children that are meant to be "protected."

Additionally, child abuse pediatricians and their hospital based teams struggle with exactly how and what their role should be. A recent study in the medical journal Pediatrics acknowledges, there is:

"*no consensus on what makes child protection teams effective.*"[2]

Since the easiest way to define "effectiveness" can often be sheer numbers, then teams who "identify" more abuse cases may be seen as more "successful" – increasing pressure to rush to judgment and quickly allege abuse.

Multiple Ethical Concerns for Child Abuse Specialists and Teams

More particularly, this new subspecialty of pediatrics has "generated questions regarding the investigatory or prosecutorial role assumed by child abuse pediatricians."[3]

A paper published last year by George Barry and Diane Redleaf of the Family Defense Center in Chicago, titled, "Medical Ethics Concerns in Physical Child Abuse Investigations,"[4] reveals the extent of breeches of medical ethics by child abuse medical investigators:

<u>*Issues That Arise As to the Child Abuse Pediatrician's Role*</u>

Most significantly, the structural issues that the child abuse pediatrics specialty gives rise to include:

- *the child abuse pediatrician not seeking out appropriate consultations with other specialists, in particular neurosurgeons and orthopedists;*

- *the child abuse pediatrician working at the same institution from which the Hotline call, that triggered the investigation, was made and in the same institution in which the child's treatment was provided, which can affect the objectivity of the child abuse pediatrician's opinion;*

- *the child abuse pediatrician failing to evaluate and weigh the information of colleagues who are treating physicians and who know the parents and family who brought the child in for treatment; and*

- *the child's treating physicians becoming passive observers, unwilling to question the opinions of the child abuse pediatrician.*

The paper concludes:

"After researching medical ethics principles and opinions as documented in this Paper, we believe that there is indeed something ethically problematic with the way the child protection community and the larger medical community, with the newly-adopted child abuse pediatrician specialty, has treated the field of child abuse investigations."

"Defensive Doctoring" Leading to Families Wrongly Accused?

Parents Claim Nationwide Children's Hospital Violated Rights After Reporting Alleged Abuse. Image from WBNS-TV, Columbus, Ohio.

Another, broader concern exhibited by child abuse pediatricians is described in social workers and judges, too:

"'Defensive social work' refers to the tendency of CPS personnel, first identified in the early 1980s, to base removal decisions on fear – fear of job discipline, fear of civil (and even criminal) liability, and especially fear of adverse publicity resulting from the death of a child left with or returned to his biological parents."

...the prevailing attitude – among the general public as well as many CPS insiders – that emergency removal is a magic bullet in the battle against child abuse and neglect, (is viewed as) a conservative, risk-free way of 'erring on the side of safety.'[5]

Disturbingly, this attitude seems to extend to child abuse pediatricians. No part of the children's hospitals' child abuse process appears to recognize, or even acknowledge, that a "defensive" rush to judgment, which some might call a "witch hunt," creates real, lasting damage in families who are wrongly accused.

A real-life example of how this plays out can be found in a federal lawsuit filed this February by seven families in Ohio against Nationwide Children's Hospital. It alleges the hospital violated a number of constitutional rights during its child abuse exams. Chad Burley, the father in one of the families, labeled it a "witch hunt."[6]

Child Abuse Pediatricians a Self-fulfilling Prophecy?

While "defensive doctoring" can reasonably describe the function of many child abuse pediatricians, another perspective raises yet more serious concerns – a self-reinforcing bias.

"I would contend the very existence of the child abuse pediatrician specialty becomes something of a self-fulfilling prophecy," notes Phil Locke of the Duke Law Wrongful Convictions Clinic. *"I'm here to diagnose child abuse, so that's what I'm going to do."*[7]

"When your tool is a hammer, the whole world is a nail," said Diana Rugh Johnson, an attorney and child-welfare law specialist in Atlanta, noting this same phenomenon.[8]

The old joke used by Howard Stern, "Have you stopped beating your wife yet?" illustrates how wrong assumptions, even in a simple question, can color people's (and doctors') perception of a situation.

The CPS system itself is built around the premise that parents – accused by anyone of anything – are "guilty until proven innocent"…an approach not terribly different from the Salem witch trials 300 years ago. And when a doctor encounters a potentially suspicious situation, he or she can easily fall into a bias that, once labeled (rightly or wrongly), can snowball.

Video Surveillance Violates Privacy Rights, Heightens Antagonism

The necessity of covert video surveillance used as a tool in identifying instances of abuse also further erodes the ethical footing of the patient-doctor relationship.

"You'd be hard pressed to find any hospital in the nation that doesn't already use some form of video surveillance," notes a practicing emergency room physician. "In fact, in the next 5-10 years I predict that audio or even video recording of patient encounters will become commonplace – much like police encounters are recorded now."[9]

Video surveillance has become an established tool for children's hospitals in identifying some forms of child abuse, particularly Munchausen syndrome by proxy (MSBP), where a caregiver is accused of deliberately causing a child's illness for personal attention.[10]

Not only is it legal, but covert video surveillance in children's hospitals is considered "a justifiable assessment tool to establish a firm diagnosis or to help to exclude deliberate harm to the child."[11]

In fact, some pediatric facilities have constructed "special inpatient rooms that are equipped with multiple cameras, all hidden and unknown to patients and family. When MSBP is suspected, the patient is transferred to that room under some pretense."[12]

Pediatric child abuse specialists, and their teams of professionals, all focused on determining guilt, are faced with multiple ethical challenges. Many feel these challenges make it almost impossible to avoid an antagonistic approach and an unbiased, medical role.

Families Irreparably Damaged, Reputations and Jobs Lost, Children Emotionally Devastated

A brief glance through MedicalKidnap.com's many stories demonstrates the horrific impact a wrongful accusation of child abuse can wreak on an innocent family. No system, and no one human being, can be perfect. But the current system at children's hospitals virtually ignores the severity of the damage that can be done when a child abuse pediatrician and the child protection team wrongly allege child abuse, creating a witch hunt with very little attention to doctors in other subspecialties or those family pediatricians with first-hand knowledge of the subjects in question.

The new children's hospitals' child abuse pediatricians and processes cannot be excused from the damages they cause, when hurting children are torn from loving and competent parents; when parents' reputations can be permanently damaged and jobs lost through state child abuse registries; and when every day a child spends in foster care represents another tick of the clock in a countdown toward termination of parental rights.

Chapter 4: From Child Protection to State-sponsored Child Kidnapping: How Did we Get Here?

When most people today hear of a terrible child abuse case, their immediate reaction is to call on the government to protect the child and bring justice to bear on the situation. This reliance upon government to enforce child protection, rather than families, churches or non-profit groups, is a relatively new concept in history.

As American government has grown ever larger in response to society's expectations that it should be all children's protector, Americans have discovered these good intentions have created a system that is becoming more and more intrusive, demanding and corrupt. Parents' protests, state hearings and local media attention are gradually bringing the public's attention to a Child Protective Services (CPS) system that has the power to rip children from their parents – and do it without any of the civil rights and protections ALL American citizens are guaranteed.

How did a government service meant to protect children become something entirely different? How and when did CPS start – and why are Americans facing its growing power without even basic civil rights?

Childhood in Ancient Times often 'Nightmarish'

The concept that children have any right to protection beyond whatever their parents do or don't provide is a relatively new concept, historically. In fact, child mortality was very high throughout much of history, and children were not treasured, as they are today, but seen as property, a commodity for barter by their fathers, and often a burden for the poor and disadvantaged.

Many ancient cultures, including the Incas, the Shang Dynasty in China, the Etruscans of present-day Italy, the Canaanites[1] and the people of Carthage, North Africa,[2] commonly sacrificed children to appease their gods and bring good fortune.

In several hundred studies published by Lloyd deMause and his associates in The Journal of Psychohistory, they have provided extensive evidence that the history of childhood has been:

"a nightmare... The further back in history one goes–and the further away from the West one gets–the more massive the neglect and cruelty one finds and the more

likely children are to have been killed, rejected, beaten, terrorized and sexually abused by their caretakers."[3]

Forced labor which was often both dangerous and required long hours, early marriages, sexual abuse of children (male and female), and brutal "discipline" in the form of beatings, starvation or worse – all these were commonplace for many children around the world.

Sadly, there are still areas of the world today where these things occur. Even in the U.S. as recently as the 1980s, doctors did not believe infants could feel pain and would perform major surgery on babies without benefit of any type of anesthesia or pain relief.[4]

Western Europe Leads World In Care for Children

The beginnings of concern for children's welfare are first noted in the 13th century in Europe, where the first child rearing tracts were published, disapproval of abandonment of children and pedophilia was expressed, and religious leaders for the first time began to warn against sexual molestation of children. The fifteenth and sixteenth centuries in Western Europe represented the great watershed — vastly improved child-rearing practices.[5] By the mid-1500s in Europe, the first legal protections from sexual abuse were offered to children.[6]

After several thousand years, societal concern was finally expressed for children's well-being. Could it be the rise of a middle class, and better prosperity in Western civilization around this time, or was it the sea-change in moral influence which coincided with the Protestant Reformation, or was it the new availability of information through the invention of the printing press? Whatever the reason, it is in Western Europe at this time that the modern CPS state can trace its roots.

'Parens Patriae' Establishes Government as "Ultimate Parent"

By early 18th century England, common law had established a legal concept called *parens patriae* – Latin for "father of the country" – identifying the king as a protector or supreme guardian of those classes threatened by forces beyond their control, particularly "charities, infants, idiots, lunatics."[7]

The concept can be found as far back as ancient Greece, when Aristotle postulated that the government has two basic powers: the police power to protect its citizens from danger and harm (known as the "police power"), and its *parens patriae* power (a later Latin term applied to this concept by Roman Law) to help those in need of parental-type care, i.e., sustenance, protection, nurturing, and education.[8]

Child protective services traces back to *parens patriae* – a legal concept still used today in the U.S. which was inherited from a time when it was assumed the king could do no wrong. Amazingly, this assumption that the state as "parent" is viewed as *capable of achieving only good* still exists giving the American CPS system virtually unlimited power with very little oversight over those it chooses to label "unfit."

Charitable Groups and Local/State Involvement

"Before the spread of nongovernmental child-protection societies beginning in 1875, intervention to protect children was sporadic, but intervention occurred. Children were not protected on the scale they are today, but adults were aware of maltreatment and tried to help,"

notes John Myers in *A Short History of Child Protection in America*.

In 1875, the first nongovernmental charitable society devoted to child protection was created, called the New York Society for the Prevention of Cruelty to Children (NYSPCC). This group is still in existence today.

Myers notes that news of the NYSPCC spread and by 1922, about 300 charitable child protection societies were scattered across America. However, for much of the twentieth century, many cities and nearly all rural areas had little or no access to formal child-protective services.

"For most abused and neglected children help came-if it came- from family and neighbors willing to get involved, from police, and from courts...The call for government child protection coincided with the increasing role of state and federal governments in social services...

During the early twentieth century, states created or strengthened state departments of welfare, social services, health, and labor. Creation of the federal Children's Bureau in 1912 broke the ice, followed by the Sheppard-Towner Act, which provided federal money from 1921 to 1929 for health services for mothers and babies."[9]

As for the federal government, prior to 1935, Washington, D.C., played an insignificant role in child welfare policy and funding.

A New Idea: Children Belong to Society First, Not Family

Increasingly in the early part of the 20th century, Americans turned to government for help with a wide variety of issues. The legal concept of *parens patriae* (government as parent) was used to establish a juvenile justice system during this time. The rise of child protection as a government responsibility coincided with this new attitude.

In 1917, an authoritative text was published for American social-service and welfare workers. *A Social History of The American Family: From Colonial Times to the Present*, by Dr. Arthur W. Calhoun stated:

"American history consummates the disappearance of the wider [or extended] familism and the substitution of the parentalism of society.... The new view is that the higher and more obligatory relation is to society rather than to the family; the family goes back to the age of savagery while the state belongs to the age of civilization. The modern individual is a world citizen, served by the world, and home interests can no longer be supreme."

This radical concept, first noted 100 years ago, has slowly crept into the heart of the U.S. legal system, with *parens patriae* as the legal tip of today's monolithic CPS system.

Federal Government Asserts Broader Rights With Children

Dorothea Lange's *Migrant Mother*

In the 1930s, the Great Depression brought about circumstances where federal government involvement in "social welfare" was welcomed. In 1935, as part of President Roosevelt's New Deal, Congress passed the Social Security Act which created old-age pensions, unemployment insurance, and vocational services, as well as Aid to Dependent Children, which provided millions of dollars to states to support poor families.

The Social Security Act authorized the Children's Bureau:

"to cooperate with state public-welfare agencies in establishing, extending, and strengthening, especially in predominantly rural areas, [child welfare services] for the protection and care of homeless, dependent, and neglected children, and children in danger of becoming delinquent."

During this time, child labor laws and compulsory school attendance laws were also enacted, again utilizing parens patriae, affirming that the government could usurp parental authority in education and labor practices.

Pediatrician Spotlights Abuse, All States Required to Establish CPS

As its preceding generation had acclimatized to federal assistance for all areas of family and home life, a new generation began to recognize child abuse as a social problem which, naturally, it expected the government to solve.

The blockbuster article *The Battered Child Syndrome* by pediatrician Henry Kempe and his colleagues in 1962 played a leading role in bringing child abuse to national attention. The medical profession and soon the media captured public and professional attention with news stories and journal articles around child abuse.

Congress responded to public concern with amendments to the Social Security Act in 1962 which required states to pledge that by 1975 they would make child welfare services available statewide. This fueled expansion of government child-welfare services, including protective services.

Warnings Surface Over Unlimited Powers of Government Child Protection

Erica Carey being arrested in California after law enforcement took her three children away from her and her husband, while they were driving back to Washington State. Photo: Courtesy KSBW, Monterey, CA.

It is at this juncture that warning voices begin to appear regarding the good intentions of those pushing for greater federal involvement in child protection.

Widely recognized psychiatrist and social critic *Dr. Thomas S.Szasz* noted:

"Under the doctrine of parens patriae... it is recognized as legitimate that, in some circumstances, people may be treated as stupid children, and the government as their wise parent... In brief, to whatever extent we bestow the power of parens patriae on the government, to that extent we grant it despotic powers. Nor can we expect that such powers, once granted to specific agencies, will remain localized. On the contrary, the process will spread, and unless halted, will envelop the state."[10]

The Modern, Federally-Funded CPS State Is Born

Yet concerns over giving unlimited power to the government, in this most precious and personal area of life, went unheeded. The federal government played a major role in shaping the nationwide system of governmental child protective services in place today through The Child Abuse Prevention and Treatment Act of 1974 (CAPTA).

Federal funds were authorized to improve states' responses to physical abuse, neglect, and sexual abuse, as CAPTA focused particular attention on improved investigation and reporting.

In addition, CAPTA marked the final passing of privately funded, nongovernmental child protection societies. Congress periodically renewed CAPTA, and this legislation remains the foundational force behind the federally-funded CPS state today.

Federal Focus Shifts from Family Reunification to Adoption

Two decades later, in an effort to avoid children languishing in foster care for years, Congress passed The Adoption and Safe Families Act of 1997 (ASFA), which was labeled by The Washington Post in January 1998 as:

"the most significant change in federal child-protection policy in almost two decades."[11]

Where once the emphasis was placed on trying to eventually reunite children with their biological parents, state and federal guidelines now favored fast-tracking adoption of children in foster care. This required a new focus on terminating the biological parents' rights.

Dorothy Roberts, a professor of law at Northwestern University and author of *Shattered Bonds: The Color of Child Welfare*, argues that ASFA is a wrong-headed assault on family preservation that goes far beyond its goal of ensuring children's safety and establishes "*a preference for adoption as the means of reducing the exploding foster care population.*"[12]

The State Owns Your Children: The Ever-Expanding Arms of CPS and Parens Patriae

"We have to break through our private idea that kids belong to parents, or kids belong to their families, and recognize that kids belong to whole communities. Once it's everyone's responsibility, and not just the household's, then we start making better investments."
https://www.youtube.com/watch?v=hAAMGatMHss

Unfortunately, while the child protection system was intended to help, Health Impact News with their "Medical Kidnap" website and other media continue to document countless abuses by the CPS system, as it grows ever more "despotic," just as Dr. Szasz predicted four decades ago.

The system no longer functions – in fact, in most cases CPS assumes that the "safest" way to handle almost any complaint it receives, based merely on any allegation, without any evidence, is to remove the child from the home.

According to Massachusetts attorney Gregory Hession:

"Many judges now believe that the government creates and grants rights, rather than preserves existing rights that are bestowed by our creator and cannot be taken away. Thus, they will ignore your parental rights if it suits them.

Judges often explain rights away if they do not favor them politically… Parents' rights to direct the upbringing of their children were never questioned until recently.

Now, the state sees itself as the parent, and it lets you have temporary custody of your own child, unless and until you do something the state doesn't like. Then the child goes back to its true parent – the state…."[13]

CPS Continues to Assert New Reasons for Child Removal

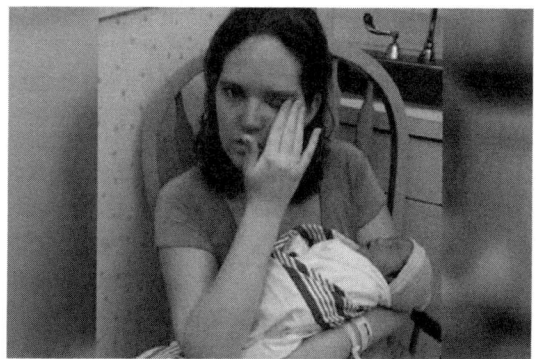

7 children including a newborn baby were seized from their parents simply because the mother had a learning disability. Verzosa family story on MedicalKidnap.com

Throughout the United States' history there has been an inexorable trend toward more and bigger government in every aspect of its citizens' lives. It's not difficult to project where the system is headed if this trend continues unchecked.

In the past few decades, *parens patriae* was used to litigate against tobacco companies and has been suggested as a basis for obesity litigation. Literally, if a child is overweight, the government may someday consider this as reason enough to remove that child from their parents.

Legal scholars admit:

"*...for much of its history as part of American jurisprudence, the boundaries and appropriate uses of parens patriae have been poorly defined.*"[14]

This is a legally open door for the government to continue to insert itself ever-more intimately in the private lives of parents and their children.

Though *parens patriae* is the historical basis for today's government involvement in parents' and children's lives, the concept that there are limits to any family's privacy and rights has moved into many other spheres in American institutions and government. Health Impact News regularly documents the many ways the medical profession has now become an arm of the government – "diagnosing" abuse, which is in fact a legal accusation, not a disease.

In yet another area of life, if a parent is disabled, the government can also use this as grounds for a child's removal.

According to a study of the National Council on Disability:

"fully two-thirds of dependency statutes allow the court to reach the determination that a parent is unfit…on the basis of the parent's disability."

Parents with disabilities face child removal rates of anywhere from 40 to 80 percent depending on the nature of their disability – far above the national norm. Those who are deaf or blind face "**extremely high rates of child removal and loss of parental rights**."

The study concludes, "*Clearly, the legal system is not protecting the rights of parents with disabilities and their children.*"[15]

Parents Without Clear Rights – CPS Can Regulate and Control Almost Anything

Additionally, legal scholars can find no "parental rights" within the Constitution. According to Parental Rights.org, federal judges are:

"citing a mounting belief that no right can be protected by the federal courts unless explicitly stated in the Constitution ... Parental rights violations are on the increase across the country, as courts exchange parental involvement for government control in the lives of America's children."

In fact, England's monarchy demonstrated where our system is headed:

"... parens patriae later evolved ... whereby the king had broad authority to regulate and control 'almost everything' that happened within his jurisdiction."[16]

Without accountability and fueled by federal money, state CPS actions may become, and some would argue already are, those of a lawless tyrant.

Despite this, a growing movement of parents, grandparents, whistleblowers, former foster children and lawyers is rallying to demand reform.

Child protection services, though intended for good, have inherited assumptions from a time when kings were thought infallible. Thomas Jefferson rightly noted:

"Experience hath shewn, that even under the best forms of government those entrusted with power have, in time, and by slow operations, perverted it into tyranny."

It is time to rein in the vague, unlimited powers of *parens patriae* – no government agency can ever replace the love and nurture of parents.

Chapter 5: Does the State Ever Have a "Right" to Remove Children from a Home?

When does the State have the right to remove children from a home where they are living with their parents?

We have been covering medical kidnapping stories now on MedicalKidnap.com for over a year. This website was started to document the many stories that were coming to our attention where families were losing their children to the State, and the foster care system, over medical disagreements. In many of these cases, their children were taken away simply because the parents disagreed with a doctor, or wanted to take their children to a different doctor to get a second opinion.

Does the State have a right to take children away from parents for what is now being called "medical abuse," a term used by medical authorities when parents disagree with doctors, or want to seek a second opinion? Most of the people who follow MedicalKidnap.com would state "no." And we have published many stories now showing that this is indeed happening all across the country, in every state, every single day.

But what about in other situations? Are there any situations in which authorities should step in and remove children from their homes, taking them away from their parents?

Judging from comments made in social media from many commenting on some of our articles, I think it is safe to assume that the majority of people in the United States today feel that in certain situations, the State has a legitimate right to step in and take children away from their families, removing them from their homes.

However, I would like to suggest that the Constitution of the United States of America protects the rights of individuals and families, and that it is never lawful for social services to remove a child from their biological parents, taking them out of their home and making them a ward of the State, removing legal custody from their parents. This phenomena is a recent development in the history of our country, and if it is not lawful to take such actions, we are correct in calling such actions "state-sponsored kidnappings."

The Bill of Rights

One of the most important legal documents in our nation's history is the first ten amendments to our nation's Constitution, known as the Bill of Rights. These "rights" were adopted during the meeting of the first U.S. Congress in 1789, and ratified by three-fourths of the state legislatures on December 15, 1791.

Here is part of the text of the Preamble, stating the purpose of these "rights":

"THE Conventions of a number of the States, having at the time of their adopting the Constitution, expressed a desire, in order to prevent misconstruction or abuse of its powers, that further declaratory and restrictive clauses should be added: And as extending the ground of public confidence in the Government, will best ensure the beneficent ends of its institution."

Clearly, the Bill of Rights, and other amendments to the U.S. Constitution that followed, were intended to protect citizens of the United States from abuses in government.

Is the removal of children from their home by force, especially in situations where neither the parents nor the children themselves want to be removed, a clear violation of the Constitution of the United States?

Again, most people would probably answer that question: only sometimes. And then the reasons people would give as to which situations children should be removed, and which situations they should not, would be hotly debated.

However, I would suggest that under the laws of the U.S. Constitution, in all situations where children are removed from their parents against the will of the parents and the children, that this is unlawful. Let's take a look at the basis of this premise.

Due Process of Law – Criminal Justice

Cornell University Law School states:

"The Constitution states only one command twice. The Fifth Amendment says to the federal government that no one shall be "deprived of life, liberty or property without due process of law." The Fourteenth Amendment, ratified in 1868, uses the same eleven words, called the Due Process Clause, to describe a legal obligation of all states. These words have as their central promise an assurance that all levels of American government must operate within the law ("legality") and provide fair procedures."[1]

The process of taking away a person's liberty or freedom, such as removing them from their home and confining them (as in a jail or prison), is known as "the criminal justice system."

Because the "due process of law" clause in the U.S. Constitution applies to all 50 states, the implementation of the criminal justice system operates very similarly in all 50 states. The criminal justice system includes law enforcement, the judicial system, and the "corrections" system.

The U.S. Constitution protects citizens from abuse of power within the criminal justice system. Here is a summary, in general, of how the system is supposed to operate within the bounds of the law set forth in the Constitution, and specifically the Bill of Rights:

Law Enforcement

1. A complaint is made against someone.

2. Law enforcement investigates the complaint to determine if there is enough evidence to support the claim. If they find evidence to support the complaint, they might make an arrest and incarcerate someone.

The Constitution sets limits to prevent abuses in power during the law enforcement process. Law enforcement cannot enter a home or private property without a warrant issued by a judge, for example. If an arrest is made, the defendant has the right to remain silent and not talk to the law enforcement officers, and the person has a right to consult with an attorney.

3. After someone is incarcerated, they must immediately be brought before a judge to press charges, and a judge must determine if there is enough evidence to hold the defendant until they can face their accusers in a trial in a court of law. If a judge determines there is enough evidence, the judge will determine if bail or bond is required to ensure the defendant appears at the trial.

Again, the Constitution was put in place to protect U.S. citizens' rights during the judicial process. They are to be given a speedy trial, and they have a right to a jury trial among their peers, for example.

4. After a trial, a person is declared guilty or innocent. If guilty, punishment is implemented.

Now, given this admittedly over-simplified summary of the criminal justice system and the protections guaranteed under the Constitution, when children are forceably removed from their home against their will or the will of their parents, based on a complaint only (such as from a physician who did not like them seeking a second opinion), is the Constitution and due process of law being followed?

Absolutely not.

Is it Legal to Forceably Remove Children from Their Parents Against their Will?

When it comes to parents and their children, why is the public today so quick to abandon the Constitution and due process of the law? Most would argue, "because the children need to be protected."

Are we so naive as to think the founders of the Constitution and legal scholars over the years did not consider cases where children were in danger within their home, so that in modern times we have to give great authority to social workers to take on this task?

Consider the case of alleged abuse in other cases where children are not involved.

For example, if there were a complaint by a woman against an alleged "abusive" husband or partner; who would be removed from the home by law enforcement if an investigation warranted it? Would the alleged victim, in this case the woman making the complaint, be the one removed from the home?

Of course not! The person the complaint was filed against would be removed, all the while having their Constitutional rights protected, by arresting them, reading their Miranda rights, and bringing them before a judge to face the charges. The alleged victim would remain in the home. That is the legal process.

But this due process of law is not followed with social services and local law enforcement when they remove children from their homes. In these cases, which we are reading increasingly in the news every day, the alleged victims are removed from the home (the children) and incarcerated, while the alleged abusers (the parents) are left in the home, and in most cases with no criminal charges filed.

This is a clear violation of the Constitution and a family's civil rights.

If you are learning about this issue for the first time, and find it hard to believe that this actually happens in the United States of America, watch this video captured by parents in a home in the Sacramento area of California, where police and CPS restrained the father outside, and then forced their way into the home (without a warrant issued by a judge) to remove an infant child from the mother's own arms, simply because they had left a hospital without a doctor's approval (who wanted to perform immediate heart surgery), and took him to a different hospital for a second opinion:

https://youtu.be/Pr1ID0CwpBU

In this unedited video, the entire incident of Child Protective Services and the Sacramento Police using force to take away Anna and Alex Nikolayev's baby is recorded. Anna and Alex had received poor care for their baby at a local hospital, and when the hospital wanted to do heart surgery on their infant, they wanted a second opinion and took the baby to a different hospital.

The first hospital did not approve of this, and did not discharge the child. Therefore, they called Child Protection Services. The parents, meanwhile, had taken the baby to a second hospital, where the child was discharged that night by a physician, since there was no immediate danger, and the surgery was not imminent.

But, the next day, Child Protection Services and the Sacramento Police showed up at the parents home to take away their baby. The husband was outside at the time, and he was forced to the ground so that the police could enter the home by force. The mother, seeing what was happening outside, set up the camera to record the whole incident (see video above).

The social workers would not even tell the mother where they were taking the baby. The police took the baby out of the mother's arms by force, and only after the social workers had already left with the baby did they allow the mother to show the police the hospital documents showing that their baby was properly discharged by a physician from the second hospital. The police did not seem to care what the facts were at all, and gave full authority to CPS to remove the child.

Why is Due Process of Law Not Followed by Child Protection Services?

The fact that the due process of law is not being followed, and that the Constitutional rights of families are clearly being violated in situations where social services removes children from the custody of their parents against their will, and against the will of the parents, is a fact that cannot be denied.

So why is it happening?

There are multiple reasons why this is happening, but they are very easy to understand.

First, when the due process of the law is followed to arrest someone, hold them in confinement, bring them before a judge to press charges, and then follow the judicial process of bringing about a "speedy trial," all of these actions are a *burden to the state*. In other words, it costs money.

When someone is arrested on suspicion of murder, rape, assault, robbery, and other serious crimes that are a threat to the public, those arrested enter into the criminal justice system, and have rights that are protected under our Constitution to ensure they are not victimized by the over-reach of government abuse.

Unfortunately, these alleged criminals are afforded more rights than parents are today, who have their children removed from their home or custody with no arrest and no trial.

One of the reasons why this is happening so frequently in the United States today is because once the children are taken into State custody, they become *an asset to the State*. What this means is that all the child's expenses are now paid via federal funds, including medical costs via Medicaid. There are also federal funds in place for foster care. The longer a child remains in State custody, the more funds that state can collect.

Secondly, when children become a ward of the State, and all of their medical bills are paid for via Medicaid, doctors are free to legally experiment on these children and include them in drug trials, without having to obtain the parents' permission. This situation is becoming so widespread, that several states are looking at adopting legislation[2] to prevent this medical experimentation from happening, including one national bill.[3]

Attorneys are Fighting Back

Attorney Shawn McMillan of California

There are attorneys all across the United States who are true family advocates, and are fighting back. Unfortunately, they are in the minority. The entire family court and juvenile court system throughout the United States employs so many judges and attorneys, attorneys who are appointed by the court to represent parents and children who cannot afford private attorneys, that there just are not enough private attorneys available to fight the current social services system taking away family rights.

Attorney Shawn McMillan of California is one such attorney, and recently he made headline news in California for filing a class action lawsuit against Riverside County in Southern California:

"Attorney McMillan is representing a federal class action lawsuit against 'Riverside County, Juvenile Dependency Investigator Karla Torres, Torres's supervisor Felicia M. Butler, and all similarly situated county social workers and investigators' for taking 'a newborn baby from her mother without a reason or a warrant,' and for making 'a habit of it.' The suit claims that the Southern California County takes 'thousands of babies' without cause."[14]

Attorney McMillan was successful in prosecuting the city of San Diego in 2014 and won a $225,000.00 lawsuit on behalf of a teenage mother who had her baby taken away illegally.

"The City of San Diego will pay $225,000 to settle a civil suit filed by a teen mom who lost parental rights to her daughter just days after the child's birth. Johnneisha Kemper says San Diego Police officers took her baby away in 2008, just days after she gave birth at the age of 16, claiming she was unfit to raise the newborn. Now, the city of San Diego has approved a settlement in the civil rights lawsuit filed alleging the SDPD took the child without threat or warrant."[5]

When Attorney McMillan approached the San Diego Police department to let them know that their actions were not legal, they allegedly responded that it did not matter, and that they would continue to seize children away from their parents under the direction of social services, and just pay the fines in court settlements like the one Mr. McMillan had just won.

Advice to Parents and Families: Know Your Constitutional Rights!

So what can parents and families do to protect themselves from unlawful seizure of their children??

The first step is to know your Constitutional rights, particularly your rights under the 5th Amendment.

One of the typical mistakes parents and family members make is to talk to social services representatives or even police if they come to your home to ask questions. Under the 5th Amendment, you do NOT have to talk to them or answer any questions, even if they come to your home with a warrant for your arrest or to search your home. Typically, an initial visit to "investigate" will not have any warrants, and in such cases you are not obligated to talk to them or let them enter your home.

In the video below, which has been viewed on YouTube in a couple of places many millions of times, Mr. James Duane, a professor at Regent Law School and a former defense attorney, tells you why you should never talk to the police under any circumstances, and that this right is protected under the 5th Amendment. Some quotes:

"I really want to do something that's been on my mind for a while, to stand up and proudly say: "God bless America, God bless the Bill of Rights, and thank God for the 5th Amendment."

I'm not ashamed to say I'm proud of the 5th Amendment, and I'm proud to admit on camera and on the Internet that I will never talk to any police officer under any circumstances.

[Let's] go to a real expert, Justice Robert Jackson, a prosecutor's prosecutor, who like me began his private practice in Buffalo, New York years before I did, and after that he served as general counsel for the Bureau of Internal Revenue, the US Department Treasury the Securities Exchange Commission assistant, the US Attorney General, and later the solicitor general and the Attorney General of the United States, and then the chief US prosecutor for the Nuremberg trials.

That's an impressive resume!

Years later, when he was a justice on the Supreme Court, just as Jackson stated: "quote any lawyer worth his salt, [he] will tell the suspect, his client, in no uncertain terms to make no statement to the police under any circumstances."

There's the title of my talk I'm here to explain to you, the surprising and somewhat counter-intuitive and admittedly unlikely reasons why Justice Jackson was right.

Do Not Talk to Police Under Any Circumstances:

https://www.youtube.com/watch?v=i8z7NC5sgik

Since we have started publishing these medical kidnapping stories, we have received many emails and comments from people who have been affected by this issue. One of them was the wife of a CPS employee who wanted us to share what she tells as many people as she can who have experienced losing their children to CPS:

"I would highly recommend that you include the following information on your pages that talk about the abuse that CPS does to families by taking children away needlessly. It will help the parents tremendously if they will hire a private lawyer. Not the court-appointed lawyer, but a private lawyer, one who knows CPS.

My husband, who works for CPS, and also recently got his master's in Social Work, said that there are virtually no children from middle and upper class families in CPS, and that the workers tremble and make sure they are careful what they do when they see a family has a private lawyer. Also, the judge is more likely to view the family favorably if he sees a private lawyer.

Many families would say or do (or neglect to say or do) things that would hurt (or help) them in their case, because they don't know the law. They will believe what they are told, even if the information is not correct, because they don't know better.

It is absolutely crucial that parents get a lawyer to help them with their case, and that they sue the agencies involved (including policemen and hospitals, if necessary) if any unlawful actions were taken against them. If the parents don't have the money, they should start a fund for friends and family and community to help them out."

A sign that can be reproduced and posted at one's home. Courtesy of Home School Legal Defense Association.
http://medicalkidnap.com/wp-content/uploads/sites/7/2014/12/searchwarrantreqd.gif

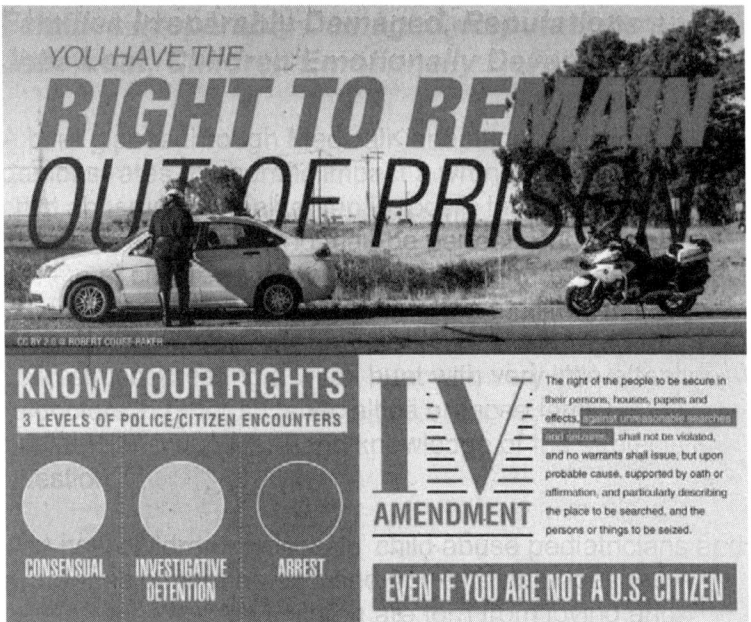

These are the Constitutional rights all suspected criminals have. Do parents have fewer rights than these? Source: Online-Paralegal-Programs.com   See the full info graphic at:
http://medicalkidnap.com/wp-content/uploads/sites/7/2015/01/know-your-rights.png

How Do We Define Parental Rights?

So how do we define "parental rights"?

This seems to be a hotly debated question on the Internet these days, especially when we publish stories of medical kidnappings.

But are "parental rights" any less than "human rights," as already defined by the Constitution of the United States of America, and specifically the Bill of Rights?

If an alleged murderer, rapist, terrorist and others are afforded due process of the law as protected under our Constitution, why not parents? Is it really lawful to allow such authority to social service workers, empowered by local law enforcement, to remove children from the custody of their parents, in cases where neither the children nor the parents agree to such separation and it must be accomplished by force against their will, with no arrest made or charges filed?

Sadly, the lawful rights of American citizens are almost never discussed in such situations in the conversations and debates we have seen in social media and the Internet when discussing these stories. Most people start with an assumption that the State has a right in some situations to forego the Constitution and due process of the law to "protect children."

Two Case Studies

Let's give two examples from stories that appeared in the mainstream media in 2015, and were highly publicized.

Meitiv Family. Image from YouTube.

The first one involved a family from Maryland. Both parents are scientists, and they follow a parenting style called "free-range" parenting. They allow their two children, ages 10 and 6, to walk together without them to places in their neighborhood, such as the neighborhood park.

Police picked them up walking home one day, due to a complaint, and CPS came in and threatened to take custody of the children, forcing the father to sign a "safety plan" they drafted. The father said he would like to consult an attorney first, and the CPS employees allegedly threatened to remove the children from the home if he did not comply. So he did.[6]

When we published this story, almost everyone wanted to debate whether or not these parents were right in allowing young children to walk the streets around their home during daylight hours.

But is that the issue we should be debating here? Was any crime committed? Were there any complaints filed against the parents that could lead to an arrest and charges pressed? The children did not file a complaint. The parents did not file a complaint. In short, were their Constitutional rights violated or not?

Yes! If we want to start judging others, based on our own interpretation of what constitutes good parenting or not, as to when the Constitution and due process of law should be abandoned, we are advocating tyranny, not rule by democratic law.

The Stanley family from Arkansas

The second case involves the Stanley family in Arkansas. Social services allegedly visited the home after an anonymous complaint. The initial visit allegedly found everything in good order, and the complaint unfounded.

However, they allegedly returned later with a search warrant for a mineral substance that the FDA has announced they think is dangerous (although not illegal). Social workers had brought a doctor to examine the children, and all were cleared with a clean bill of health. Nevertheless, after searching the home for 5 hours and interviewing all 7 children, the children were removed from the home, against their will (or at least most of them) and the will of their parents.

After the children had been taken into custody, with no charges filed against the parents, the sheriff issued a press release stating that the children were being held under charges of "abuse," and not due to the mineral supplement mentioned in the warrant. But no complaint was filed, and no arrest was made. It was later revealed that some of the older children, including one who does not live with the family any longer, do not apparently agree with the parents' religious views or parenting style.

Again, almost all of the conversation or debating involving this story was around whether or not the children were in danger and should have been removed. Were the parents and younger children's Constitutional rights violated?

Yes! Once again, due process of law was not followed, and the alleged victims, the younger children, were allegedly traumatized by being forceably removed from their parents against their will, and the will of their parents.

Whether or not the parents did "abuse" their children is not the main issue here, but whether or not there was reason to abandon due process of the law, and Constitutional rights. If we afford due process of law and civil rights to alleged murderers, rapists, terrorists, and others (who can also be a threat to children), then why not to parents? Why can't the alleged "abuser" be removed from the home, arrested, and charged with a crime, instead of removing the alleged victims and traumatizing them? (We actually answer this question above.)

In both these cases, if the State acted outside the bounds of the law and the family's Constitutional rights were violated, it is properly called "state-sponsored kidnapping." Also, in both cases, the parents could have acted more wisely to try to prevent these state-sponsored kidnappings by understanding their Constitutional rights, and refusing to talk to the social workers and police the first time they showed up.

Of course with medical kidnappings, as can be seen above in the case with baby Sammy and the parents in Sacramento, it is almost impossible today to refuse the complaint of a medical authority if one takes their child to a medical facility, and disagrees with the "Holy Doctors" who are worshiped much like deities in our culture today.

If we are going to change this system of tyranny involving state-sponsored kidnappings, we must wise up and understand what due process of law means, and what our rights are under the Constitution and Bill of Rights. We must STOP debating the merits of each of these state-sponsored kidnappings, and understand that if due process of the law is violated, then they are ALL wrong.

Here at the beginning of 2016, the parents in both of these stories have begun lawsuits against the entities that kidnapped their children illegally. Unfortunately, many of the parents in these stories do not have the financial resources to take this kind of legal action.

Who Will Stand up for Parental Rights?

As we asked above, are "parental rights" really any less than all basic "human rights" afforded to citizens of the United States under the Constitution? Do parents have less rights than suspected murderers, rapists, terrorists, etc.? If the Bill of Rights and the Constitution of the United States protect suspected criminals from abuse of government power, do not those same rights apply to parents who are accused of being "abusive"? Does the State ever have a right to remove children from their family without following the same due process of law applied to others suspected of criminal activity?

Sadly, one group that would like to be known as a national group standing for "Parental Rights" apparently feels the State has a right to take children away from their parents if those parents are seen as "unfit." In a discussion about the Stanley Family story in Arkansas on their Facebook page, they made the following statement after the sheriff's department issued their statement to the press on alleged abuses by the parents, as a reason for why they removed the children from the family:

"While we stand by the right of fit parents to make decisions for their children, there are also times when the state must intervene where parents have been abusive or

negligent." (Popular National Parental Rights Organization)
-

Does this statement sound like it comes from a group that wants to defend the Constitution and the Bill of Rights, protecting "parental rights"? As of the time of this writing, there still have been no formal charges made, nor arrests made, with either parent of the Stanley Family, and yet this "Parental Rights" group believes that the State's actions are legitimate if the parents are "abusive or negligent" by someone's standards of "fit" or "unfit" parents.

Unfortunately, that is called "tyranny" or "fascism," and such abuse of civil rights is why our founding fathers wrote the Constitution and added the Bill of Rights.

It would appear to me, that most Americans have lost their way in understanding these important liberties that so many have sacrificed their lives to defend. Until we decide to stand up for these rights that are written into the Constitution of the United States of America, don't expect much to change. Many brave men and women have given up their very lives to protect these rights, and we should not give them up so easily.

Chapter 6: A Tribute to Senator Nancy Schaefer – Exposing State-sponsored Kidnappings

Georgia Senator Nancy Schaefer. Image from We Demand An Extensive Investigation On The Death Of Senator Nancy Schaefer Facebook Page.

Georgia Senator Nancy Schaefer may have known more about State-sponsored kidnappings than any other politician in the United States before she was murdered in March of 2010. Her published report, *The Corrupt Business of Child Protective Services*, is reproduced below. It was the basis for many lectures and interviews she gave on the topic. She claims the report caused her to lose her Senate seat in the Georgia State Senate, but she stated:

"However, there are causes worth losing over."

This cause was so big however, that there are some who believe she lost more than just her job. They believe she lost her very life.

On March 26, 2010, police from Habersham County, Georgia reported that they found Nancy Schaefer and her husband, Bruce Schaefer, dead in their home. The official report was that it was a murder-suicide, and that Bruce Schaefer had killed his wife and then turned his .38-caliber handgun on himself. Their daughter reportedly found them in their bedroom, and investigators say they discovered a suicide note, as well as notes to each of the couple's five children.

However, many have questioned the "official" police report. Mark Davis of The Atlanta Journal-Constitution published an article on April 4, 2010 titled:

What really took 2 lives in Schaefer case?[1]

Some excerpts from Mark Davis' article:

And yet, people talk. They talk about a twosome that was rarely apart, about a woman who achieved renown for her unapologetic stands against abortion and overzealous child protective services.

"You hardly ever saw one without the other," said Robert "Buster" Smith, whom Bruce often visited when Nancy came to town from their Clarkesville home to get her hair done.

A Toccoa native, Smith saw Bruce Schaefer on the last Tuesday of his life when he stopped by Smith's furniture store. "He seemed like his old self," said Smith. "I have a hard time believing it happened like it happened."

Nancy Schaefer was a former officer of the Georgia Baptist Convention, and the Baptist Press also ran a piece on the murder:

Nancy Schaefer, conservative activist, killed [2]

They also raised the question as to whether the police report was accurate:

However, at least one friend of the Schaefers has questioned the murder-suicide theory. Garland Favorito, founder of Voters Organized for Trusted Election Results in Georgia (VoterGA), circulated an 11-point, two-page bulletin via the Internet stating it is "more obvious" that the case is a "murder made to look like suicide."

Favorito cited the Christian faith and pro-life beliefs of the Schaefers and the fact that Nancy Schaefer had been delving into alleged corruption in family & child services agencies.

I looked up Garland Favorito's bulletin and found it online.[3] Here is what he wrote:

Although off topic, I felt led to do one more update on the Schaefer family with some new information. I want to particularly thank the progressives and Democrats who responded with encouragement to my previous article by recognizing that the child abuse and trafficking against which Sen. Schaefer fought for the last two years of her life is a non-partisan issue that transcends political party boundaries.

On Wed. Mar 31, over 1000 people flocked to Ebenezer Baptist Church in Toccoa Ga. to pay last respects to former state senator, Nancy Schaefer and husband, Bruce. Pastor Andy Childs focused on the forgiveness of sins and eternal life available to all mankind through Jesus Christ. He felt they would have wanted it that way. Pastor Childs also mentioned that he researched Nancy Schaefer's efforts in Child Protective Services, which I believe will eventually become her legacy and greatest work.

Many people in line and at the service who knew Bruce "Bear" Schaefer were still consumed with doubt that he would do something so uncharacteristic as to kill his wife and himself. More information is gradually coming to light about the couple's financial troubles that may have led to the tragedy but several points have fostered doubt:

The Schaefer's were receiving death threats that had accelerated;
There was no indication from Bruce Schaefer of him being under any kind of stress that would cause him to commit such an uncharacteristic act right up to the eve of their death;
Nancy Schaefer was completing a video exposing the lack of oversight in Georgia's Department of Family and Child Services (DFCS) as well as Child Protective Services (CPS) nationally.
I spoke at some length with the video producer, William "Wilky" Fain. Both he and other friends of the family corroborate that Bruce had complained of investment losses and they had just received a foreclosure notice on the magnificent home they owned. They had put their home up for sale a couple months earlier but had been unable to sell it or another property in such a down market.

Still, many of the couple's friends question whether their financial condition was really severe enough to warrant such an uncharacteristic drastic action. Burning psychological questions remain such as:

1. Why would Bruce decide to kill himself and his wife because he received a foreclosure notice on a home that they had already decided to sell two months earlier?

2. Why would Bruce consider the couple's financial situation so severe when their assets still appeared to exceed their secured property debt by several hundred thousand dollars?

3. If Bruce was under financial stress, why did he not show any signs of it up to an including the eve of the couple's death?

4. If Bruce was under financial stress why wouldn't he seek help from any or all of his five grown children who loved him and would have wanted to help?

5. Why would Bruce decide to deprive both he and Nancy of seeing the grandchildren who they loved so dearly grow up?

6. Why would Bruce knowingly take a drastic action that would devastate the children and grandchildren who loved him so much?

7. Why would Bruce, who was so highly supportive of Nancy's efforts for decades, including her CPS/DFCS work, decide to kill her just at the peak of one of her most important works?

8. Why would Bruce commit such an act that was so against his faith and completely out of character for him according to those who know him best?

9. Why would Bruce jeopardize any chance of the family collecting life insurance benefits by committing suicide and killing his wife?

One of Nancy Schaefer's Last Interviews

Less than a year before she was murdered, Nancy Schaefer appeared on the Alex Jones show to discuss the American foster care and adoption business, and the terrible corruption involved with it, including "bounties" on children and child sex trafficking. Her interview is available via YouTube.

Part 1

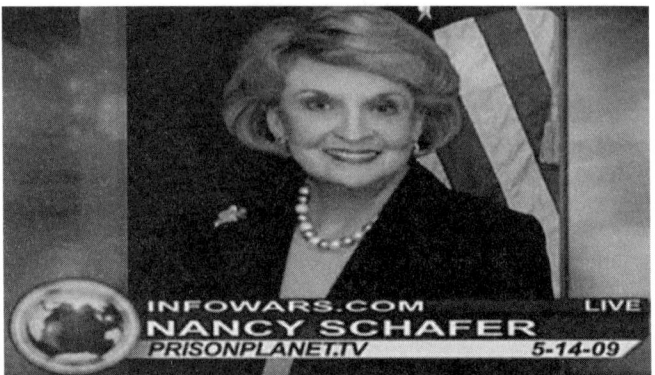

https://www.youtube.com/watch?v=yhzu80PfUKU

Excerpts from Part 1 of the interview:

Nancy Schaefer says that CPS is unconstitutional.

Parents across this country need to be warned of the dangers of Child Protection Services nationwide.

"The Department of Child Protective Services has become a protected empire. It's built on taking children and separating families."

After she lost her State Senate seat due to what she believes was her report on CPS, she began to talk to other State Representatives and Senators around the country who were being confronted with CPS issues in their district, but they told her that if they did anything, they would lose their jobs just as Nancy Schaefer had.

Alex Jones asked her if there were "bounties on the heads of children" and Mrs. Schaefer said "yes," and that in fact just the day before she had learned that "an order" had come in to a CPS office stating what kind of child someone wanted to adopt.

Mrs. Schaefer states that the financial motive for the State to legally kidnap children was put in place in 1974 by Walter Mondale with the "Adoption and Safe Families Act." This was later expanded by President Bill Clinton in 1997 with The Adoption and Safe Families Act that gave states cash bonuses for every child adopted out of foster care. (Note: Bill Clinton signed this bill into law, but the bill was passed by the Republican-led House and Senate led by Newt Gingrich, so it was a bi-partisan effort initiated by a Republican majority in Congress.)

Part 2

https://www.youtube.com/watch?v=tA-wE6VgRek

Excerpts from Part 2 of the interview:

In this segment, Mrs. Schaefer talks about how States have a "base formula" regarding how much each child is worth in terms of collecting federal funding, and how they can increase that formula to get all the federal funding that is available. If they get close to the end of the year and they have not collected all the funds available for that State, there is more incentive to put more children into foster care.

Mrs. Schaefer explained how the words "in the best interest of the child" have been redefined by CPS, whose goal is to destroy the family. She explained how grandparents often cannot even get custody of their own grandchildren when it would be in the best interest of the children to be with their grandparents. She explained how children are much more likely to be abused in foster care than they are when they are left with "abusive" parents.

She gives first hand experience of a case in her district where two little girls were removed from their mother because the mother allegedly had an unopened can of beer in her car, and the girls were placed into a foster home with many other children where they were sexually abused, including by the CPS caseworker who lived in the foster home.

Part 3

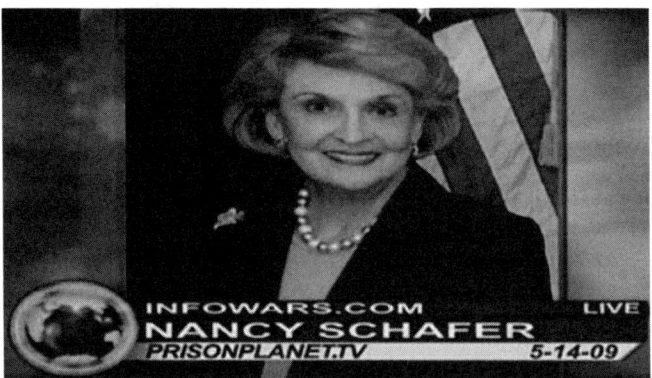

https://www.youtube.com/watch?v=gF7qNmqJ670

Excerpts from Part 3 of the interview:

In this third segment, Mrs. Schaefer finishes the story of how she became exposed to the corruption in CPS, with a grandmother in Florida who was trying to get custody of her grandchildren in Georgia, which is the story started in the previous section. She persisted with the help of Senator Schaefer, and eventually was able to get custody of her grandchildren, but then the juvenile court judge issued an order for the girls to become the custody of their biological father who lived on the West Coast, but had never been a part of their lives. He reportedly was in the business of "Adult Entertainment," which included pornography according to Mrs. Schaefer.

Both Alex Jones and Senator Schaefer comment on how many pedophiles are involved in social services like CPS working with children.

Mrs. Schaefer again reiterates that the system has to be exposed and completely dissolved. All federal funding needs to be cut off, and the rescuing of truly abused children in homes needs to become the function of law enforcement, and not social workers. This would provide due process of law. This mantra of hers to cut off funding and expose everything certainly provided a motive for someone to not want her doing that job.

One of the tragic things Mrs. Schaefer said in this segment was that she was overwhelmed with calls from families losing their children all across the U.S., and they had no where to turn for justice. "There is no where to go," she stated. Our own experience here at MedicalKidnap.com since launching our website reflects this.

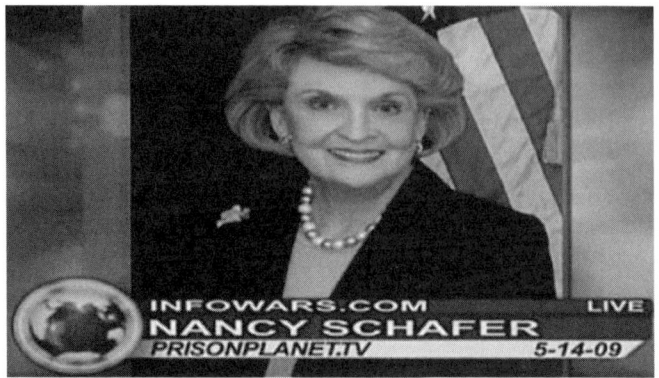

https://www.youtube.com/watch?v=dNvG_fl2o3s

Excerpts from Part 4 of the interview:

In this last segment, Alex Jones asked the Senator how to fight this corruption. Mrs. Schaefer replied that she tried to pass a bill in Georgia that would have helped to stop it, but it was defeated. She mentioned the incredible bureaucracy that exists in the system, and all the jobs that "child protection services" provided, which is a huge "business."

Here is the published report Nancy Schaefer did on CPS.

The Corrupt Business of Child Protective Services

By Nancy Schaefer Senator
50th District Georgia

https://www.youtube.com/watch?v=u5fqaaBpTLY

My introduction into child protective service cases was due to a grandmother in an adjoining state who called me with her tragic story. Her two granddaughters had been taken from her daughter who lived in my district. Her daughter was told wrongly that if she wanted to see her children again she should sign a paper and give up her children. Frightened and young, the daughter did. I have since discovered that parents are often threatened into cooperation of permanent separation of their children.

The children were taken to another county and placed in foster care. The foster parents were told wrongly that they could adopt the children. The grandmother then jumped through every hoop known to man in order to get her granddaughters. When the case finally came to court it was made evident by one of the foster parent's children that the foster parents had, at any given time, 18 foster children and that the foster mother had an inappropriate relationship with the caseworker.

In the courtroom, the juvenile judge acted as though she was shocked and said the two girls would be removed quickly. They were not removed. Finally, after much pressure being applied to the Department of Family and Children Services of Georgia (DFCS), the children were driven to South Georgia to meet their grandmother who gladly drove to meet them. After being with their grandmother two or three days, the judge, quite out of the blue, wrote up a new order to send the girls to their father, who previously had no interest in the case and who lived on the West Coast. The father was in "adult entertainment." His girlfriend worked as an "escort" and his brother, who also worked in the business, had a sexual charge brought against him.

Within a couple of days the father was knocking on the grandmother's door and took the girls kicking and screaming to California.

The father developed an unusual relationship with the former foster parents and soon moved back to the southeast, and the foster parents began driving to the father's residence and picking up the little girls for visits. The oldest child had told her mother and grandmother on two different occasions that the foster father molested her.

To this day after five years, this loving, caring blood relative grandmother does not even have visitation privileges with the children. The little girls are in my opinion permanently traumatized and the young mother of the girls was so traumatized with shock when the girls were first removed from her that she has not recovered.

Throughout this case and through the process of dealing with multiple other mismanaged cases of the Department of Family and Children Services (DFCS), I have worked with other desperate parents and children across the state because they have no rights and no one with whom to turn. I have witnessed ruthless behavior from many caseworkers, social workers, investigators, lawyers, judges, therapists, and others such as those who "pick up" the children. I have been stunned by what I have seen and heard from victims all over the state of Georgia.

In this report, I am focusing on the Georgia Department of Family and Children Services (DFCS). However, I believe Child Protective Services nationwide has become corrupt and that the entire system is broken almost beyond repair.

I am convinced parents and families should be warned of the dangers.

The Department of Child Protective Services, known as the Department of Family and Children Service (DFCS) in Georgia and other titles in other states, has become a "protected empire" built on taking children and separating families. This is not to say that there are not those children who do need to be removed from wretched situations and need protection. This report is concerned with the children and parents caught up in "legal kidnapping," ineffective policies, and DFCS who do does not remove a child or children when a child is enduring torment and abuse. – (See Exhibit A and Exhibit B)

In one county in my District, I arranged a meeting for thirty-seven families to speak freely and without fear. These poor parents and grandparents spoke of their painful, heart wrenching encounters with DFCS. Their suffering was overwhelming. They wept and cried. Some did not know where their children were and had not seen them in years. I had witnessed the "Gestapo" at work and I witnessed the deceitful conditions under which children were taken in the middle of the night, out of hospitals, off of school buses, and out of homes. In one county a private drug testing business was operating within the DFCS department that required many, many drug tests from parents and individuals for profit. In another county children were not removed when they were enduring the worst possible abuse. Due to being exposed, several employees in a particular DFCS office were fired. However, they have now been rehired either in neighboring counties or in the same county again. According to the calls I am now receiving, the conditions in that county are returning to the same practices that they had before the light was shown on their deeds. Having worked with probably 300 cases statewide, I am convinced there is no responsibility and no accountability in the system.

I have come to the conclusion:

- that poor parents often times are targeted to lose their children because they do not have the where-with-all to hire lawyers and fight the system. Being poor does not mean you are not a good parent or that you do not love your child, or that your child should be removed and placed with strangers;

- that all parents are capable of making mistakes and that making a mistake does not mean your children are always to be removed from the home. Even if the home is not perfect, it is home; and that's where a child is the safest and where he or she wants to be, with family;

- that parenting classes, anger management classes, counseling referrals, therapy classes and on and on are demanded of parents with no compassion by the system even while they are at work and while their children are separated from them. This can take months or even years and it emotionally devastates both children and parents. Parents are victimized by "the system" that makes a profit for holding children longer and "bonuses" for not returning children;

- that caseworkers and social workers are oftentimes guilty of fraud. They withhold evidence. They fabricate evidence and they seek to terminate parental rights. However, when charges are made against them, the charges are ignored;

- that the separation of families is growing as a business because local governments have grown accustomed to having taxpayer dollars to balance their ever-expanding budgets;

- that Child Protective Service and Juvenile Court can always hide behind a confidentiality clause in order to protect their decisions and keep the funds flowing. There should be open records and "court watches"! Look who is being paid! There are state employees, lawyers, court investigators, court personnel, and judges. There are psychologists, and psychiatrists, counselors, caseworkers, therapists, foster parents, adoptive parents, and on and on. All are looking to the children in state custody to provide job security. Parents do not realize that social workers are the glue that holds "the system" together that funds the court, the child's attorney, and the multiple other jobs including DFCS's attorney.

- that The Adoption and the Safe Families Act, set in motion by President Bill Clinton, offered cash "bonuses" to the states for every child they adopted out of foster care. In order to receive the "adoption incentive bonuses" local child protective services need more children. They must have merchandise (children) that sell and you must have plenty of them so the buyer can choose. Some counties are known to give a $4,000 bonus for each child adopted and an additional $2,000 for a "special needs" child. Employees work to keep the federal dollars flowing;

- that there is double dipping. The funding continues as long as the child is out of the home. When a child in foster care is placed with a new family then "adoption bonus funds" are available. When a child is placed in a mental health facility and is on 16 drugs per day, like two children of a constituent of mine, more funds are involved;

- that there are no financial resources and no real drive to unite a family and help keep them together;

- that the incentive for social workers to return children to their parents quickly after taking them has disappeared and who in protective services will step up to the plate and say, "This must end!" No one, because they are all in the system together and a system with no leader and no clear policies will always fail the children. Look at the waste in government that is forced upon the taxpayer;

- that the "Policy Manual" is considered "the last word" for DFCS. However, it is too long, too confusing, poorly written and does not take the law into consideration;

- that if the lives of children were improved by removing them from their homes, there might be a greater need for protective services, but today all children are not always safer. Children, of whom I am aware, have been raped and impregnated in foster care and the head of a Foster Parents Association in my District was recently arrested because of child molestation;

- that some parents are even told if they want to see their children or grandchildren, they must divorce their spouse. Many, who are under privileged, feeling they have no option, will divorce and then just continue to live together. This is an anti-family policy, but parents will do anything to get their children home with them.

- fathers, (non-custodial parents) I must add, are oftentimes treated as criminals without access to their own children and have child support payments strangling the very life out of them;

- that the Foster Parents Bill of Rights does not bring out that a foster parent is there only to care for a child until the child can be returned home. Many Foster Parents today use the Foster Parent Bill of Rights to hire a lawyer and seek to adopt the child from the real parents, who are desperately trying to get their child home and out of the system;

- that tax dollars are being used to keep this gigantic system afloat, yet the victims, parents, grandparents, guardians and especially the children, are charged for the system's services.

- that grandparents have called from all over the State of Georgia trying to get custody of their grandchildren. DFCS claims relatives are contacted, but there are cases that prove differently. Grandparents who lose their grandchildren to strangers have lost their own flesh and blood. The children lose their family heritage and grandparents, and parents too, lose all connections to their heirs.

- that The National Center on Child Abuse and Neglect in 1998 reported that six times as many children died in foster care than in the general public and that once removed to official "safety," these children are far more likely to suffer abuse, including sexual molestation than in the general population.

- That according to the California Little Hoover Commission Report in 2003, 30% to 70% of the children in California group homes do not belong there and should not have been removed from their homes.

FINAL REMARKS

On my desk are scores of cases of exhausted families and troubled children. It has been beyond me to turn my back on these suffering, crying, and sometimes beaten down individuals. We are mistreating the most innocent. Child Protective Services have become adult centered to the detriment of children. No longer is judgment based on what the child needs or who the child wants to be with or what is really best for the whole family; it is some adult or bureaucrat who makes the decisions, based often on just hearsay, without ever consulting a family member, or just what is convenient, profitable, or less troublesome for a director of DFCS.

I have witnessed such injustice and harm brought to these families that I am not sure if I even believe reform of the system is possible! The system cannot be trusted. It does not serve the people. It obliterates families and children simply because it has the power to do so. Children deserve better. Families deserve better. It's time to pull back the curtain and set our children and families free.

"Speak up for those who cannot speak for themselves, for the rights of all who are destitute.

Speak up and judge fairly; defend the rights of the poor and the needy." Proverbs 31:8-9

RECOMMENDATIONS

1. Call for an independent audit of the Department of Family and Children's Services (DFCS) to expose corruption and fraud.

2. Activate immediate change. Every day that passes means more families and children are subject to being held hostage.

3. End the financial incentives that separate families.

4. Grant to parents their rights in writing.

5. Mandate a search for family members to be given the opportunity to adopt their own relatives.

6. Mandate a jury trial where every piece of evidence is presented before removing a child from his or her parents.

7. Require a warrant or a positive emergency circumstance before removing children from their parents. (Judge Arthur G. Christean, Utah Bar Journal, January, 1997 reported that "except in emergency circumstances, including the need for immediate medical care, require warrants upon affidavits of probable cause before entry upon private property is permitted for the forcible removal of children from their parents.")

8. Uphold the laws when someone fabricates or presents false evidence. If a parent alleges fraud, hold a hearing with the right to discovery of all evidence.

Senator Nancy Schaefer

50th District of Georgia

EXHIBIT A

December 5, 2006
Jeremy's Story

(Some names withheld due to future hearings.)
As told to Senator Nancy Schaefer by Sandra (XXXX), a foster parent of Jeremy for 2 +½ years.

My husband and I received Jeremy when he was 2 weeks old and we have been the only parents he has really ever known. He lived with us for 27 months. (XXXX) is the grandfather of Jeremy, and he is known for molesting his own children, for molesting Jeremy and has been court ordered not to be around Jeremy. (XXXX) is the mother of Jeremy, who has been diagnosed to be mentally ill, and also is known to have molested Jeremy. (XXXX) and Jeremy's uncle is a registered sex offender and (XXXX) is the biological father, who is a drug addict and alcoholic and who continues to be in and out of jail. Having just described Jeremy's world, all of these adults are not to be any part of Jeremy's life, yet for years DFCS has known that they are. DFCS had to test (XXXX) (the grandfather) and his son (XXXX) (the uncle) and (XXXX) to determine the real father. (XXXX) is the biological father although any of them might have been. In court, it appeared from the case study, that everyone involved knew that this little boy had been molested by family members, even by his own mother, (XXXX). In court, (XXX), the mother of Jeremy, admitted to having had sex with (XXXX) (the grandfather) and (XXXX) (her own brother) that morning. Judge (XXXX) and DFCS gave Jeremy to his grandmother that same day. (XXXX), the grandmother, is over 300 lbs., is unable to drive, and is unable to take care of Jeremy due to physical problems. She also has been in a mental hospital several times due to her behavior. Even though it was ordered by the court that the grandfather (XXXX), the uncle (XXXX) (a convicted sex offender), (XXXX) his mother who molested him and (XXXX) his biological father, a convicted drug addict, were not to have anything to do with the child, they all continue to come and go as they please at (XXXX address), where Jeremy has been sentenced to live for years. This residence has no bathroom and little heat. The front door and the windows are boarded. (See pictures) This home should have been condemned years ago. I have been in this home. No child should ever have to live like this or with such people. Jeremy was taken from us at age 2 +½ years after (XXXX) obtained attorney (XXXX), who was the same attorney who represented him in a large settlement from an auto accident. I am told, that attorney (XXXX), as grandfather's attorney, is known to have repeatedly gotten (XXXX) off of several criminal charges in White County. This is a matter of record and is known by many in White County. I have copies of some records. (XXXX grandfather), through (XXXX attorney's) work, got (XXXX), the grandmother of Jeremy, legal custody of Jeremy. (XXXX grandfather) who cannot read or write also got his daughter (XXXX) and son (XXXX) diagnosed by government agencies as mentally ill. (XXXX grandfather), through legal channels, has taken upon himself all control of the family and is able to take possession of any government funding coming to these people.

It was during this time that Jeremy was to have a six-month transitional period between (XXXX grandmother) and my family as we were to give him up. The court ordered agreement was to have been 4 days at our house and 3 days at (XXXX grandmother). DFCS stopped the visits within 2 weeks. The reason given by DFCS was the child was too traumatized going back and forth. In truth, Jeremy begged us and screamed never to be taken back to (XXXX his grandmother) house, which we have on video. We, as a family, have seen Jeremy in stores time to time with (XXXX grandmother) and the very people he is not to be around. At each meeting Jeremy continues to run to us wherever he sees us and it is clear he is suffering. This child is in a desperate situation and this is why I am writing, and begging you Senator Schaefer, to do something in this child's behalf. Jeremy can clearly describe in detail his sexual molestation by every member of this family and this sexual abuse continues to this day.

When Jeremy was 5 years of age I took him to Dr. (XXXX) of Habersham County who did indeed agree that Jeremy's rectum was black and blue and the physical damage to the child was clearly a case of sexual molestation.

Early in Jeremy's life, when he was in such bad physical condition, we took him to Egleston Children Hospital where at two months of age therapy was to begin three times a week. DFCS decided that the (XXXX grandparent family) should participate in his therapy. However, the therapist complained over and over that the (XXXX grandparent family) would not even wash their hands and would cause Jeremy to cry during these sessions. (XXXX the grandmother), after receiving custody no longer allowed the therapy because it was an inconvenience. The therapist reported that this would be a terrible thing to do to this child. Therapy was stopped and it was detrimental to the health of Jeremy. During (XXXX grandmother) custody, (XXXX uncle) has shot Jeremy with a BB gun and there is a report at (XXXX) County Sheriff's office. There are several amber alerts at Cornelia Wal-Mart, Commerce Wal-Mart, and a 911 report from (XXXX) County Sheriff's Department when Jeremy was lost. (XXXX grandmother), to teach Jeremy a lesson, took thorn bush limbs and beat the bottoms of his feet. Jeremy's feet got infected and his feet had to be lanced by Dr. (XXXX). Then Judy called me to pick him up after about 4 days to take back him to the doctor because of intense pain. I took Jeremy to Dr. (XXXX) in Gainesville. Dr. (XXXX) said surgery was needed immediately and a cast was added. After returning home, (XXXX), his grandfather and (XXXX), his uncle, took him into the hog lot and allowed him to walk in the filth.

Jeremy's feet became so infected for a 2nd time that he was again taken back to Dr. (XXXX) and the hospital. No one in the hospital could believe this child's living conditions. Jeremy is threatened to keep quiet and not say anything to anyone. I have videos, reports, arrest records and almost anything you might need to help Jeremy. Please call my husband, Wendell, or me at any time.

Sandra and (XXXX) husband (XXXX)

EXHIBIT B

Failure of DFCS to remove six desperate children

A brief report regarding six children that Habersham County DFCS director failed to remove as disclosed to Senator Nancy Schaefer by Sheriff Deray Fincher of Habersham County.

Sheriff Deray Fincher, Chief of Police Don Ford and Chief Investigator Lt. Greg Bowen Chief called me to meet with them immediately, which I did on Tuesday, October 16, 2007. Sheriff Fincher, after contacting the Director of Habersham County DFCS several times to remove six children from being horribly abused, finally had to get a court order to remove the children himself with the help of two police officers.

The children, four boys and two girls, were not just being abused; they were being tortured by a monster father.

The six children and a live in girl friend were terrified of this man, the abuser. The children never slept in a bed, but always on the floor. The place where they lived was unfit for human habitation.

The father on one occasion hit one of the boys across his head with a bat and cut the boy's head open. The father then proceeded to hold the boy down and sew up the child's head with a needle and red thread. However, even with beatings and burnings, this is only a fraction of what the father did to these children and to the live-in girlfriend.

Sheriff Fincher has pictures of the abuse and condition of one of the boys and at the writing of this report, he has the father in jail in Habersham County.

It should be noted that when the DFCS director found out that Sheriff Fincher was going to remove the children, she called the father and warned him to flee.

This is not the only time this DFCS director failed to remove a child when she needed to do so. (See Exhibit A)

The egregious acts and abhorrent behavior of officials who are supposed to protect children can no longer be tolerated.

Senator Nancy Schaefer
50th District of Georgia

References

Chapter 1 – Medical Kidnapping: A Threat to Every Child in America Today

1. United States Senate – PERMANENT SUBCOMMITTEE ON INVESTIGATIONS - Committee on Homeland Security and Governmental Affairs – Rob Portman, Chairman – *Protecting Unaccompanied Alien Children from Trafficking and Other Abuses: The Role of the Office of Refugee Resettlement*
http://www.portman.senate.gov/public/index.cfm/files/serve?File_id=ad5834df-8f8a-4fe5-aa34-a7ab64dfd288

Chapter 2: Medical Kidnapping in the U.S. – Kidnapping Children for Drug Trials

1. Carl L. Tishler, PhD, Natalie Staats Reiss, PhD; "Pediatric Drug-Trial Recruitment: Enticement Without Coercion," Pediatrics, Vol. 127 No. 5, May 1, 2011, pp. 949-954, doi: 10.1542/peds.2010-2585.
http://pediatrics.aappublications.org/content/127/5/949.full

2. IBID.

3. "Protections for Foster Children Enrolled in Clinical Trials," Hearing before the Subcommittee on Human Resources of the Committee on Ways and Means, U.S. House of Representatives, First Session of the One Hundred ninth Congress, May 18, 2005, Serial No. 109-8.
http://www.gpo.gov/fdsys/pkg/CHRG-109hhrg36660/html/CHRG-109hhrg36660.htm

4. "Report Exposes Why Corrupt CPS Agencies Seldom Place Foster Children with Family Members," MedicalKidnap.com, 5/6/2015.
http://medicalkidnap.com/2015/05/06/report-exposes-why-

corrupt-cps-agencies-seldom-place-foster-children-with-family-members/

5. Joseph J. Doyle, Jr., "Child Protection and Child Outcomes: Measuring the Effects of Foster Care," Sloan School of Management, Massachusetts Institute of Technology, 2007 (Study)

6. "A History of Medical Kidnapping at Phoenix Children's Hospital," MedicalKidnap.com, 10/14/2014. http://medicalkidnap.com/2014/10/14/a-history-of-medical-kidnapping-at-phoenix-childrens-hospital/

7. "Senator Nancy Schaefer: Did her Fight Against CPS Child Kidnapping Cause her Murder?" Health Impact News, 2015. http://healthimpactnews.com/2015/senator-nancy-schaefer-did-her-fight-against-cps-child-kidnapping-cause-her-murder/

8. "Is Foster Care "In the Best Interest of the Child"?" MedicalKidnap.com, 5/9/2015. http://medicalkidnap.com/2015/05/09/is-foster-care-in-the-best-interest-of-the-child/

9. "Protections for Foster Children Enrolled in Clinical Trials," Hearing before the Subcommittee on Human Resources of the Committee on Ways and Means, U.S. House of Representatives, First Session of the One Hundred ninth Congress, May 18, 2005, Serial No. 109-8. http://www.gpo.gov/fdsys/pkg/CHRG-109hhrg36660/html/CHRG-109hhrg36660.htm

10. IBID.

11. Clinical Trials Register, Retrieved 5/15/2015. https://www.clinicaltrialsregister.eu/ctr-search/search;jsessionid=Y2ZFZbnI53-Xs10DdRlPUPD54hjV1kBA5iOcUrr3WwPJKbGpTfHV!-3122046

Chapter 3: Are New Pediatric "Child Abuse Specialists" Causing an Increase in Medical Kidnappings?

1. https://www.childrenshospitals.org/issues-and-advocacy/child-health/child-abuse/fact-sheets/child-abuse-facts-and-trends from the Children's Hospital Association, March 20, 2015

2. Study in Pediatrics, July, 2010
http://www.ncbi.nlm.nih.gov/pmc/articles/PMC3596017/

3. "Litigating Shaken Baby Syndrome Allegations in the Child Welfare Context," by Melissa L. Staas, June 18, 2015
http://apps.americanbar.org/litigation/committees/childrights/content/articles/summer2015-0615-litigating-sbs-allegations-child-welfare-context.html

4. "MEDICAL ETHICS CONCERNS IN PHYSICAL CHILD ABUSE INVESTIGATIONS: A CRITICAL PERSPECTIVE," by George J. Barry and Diane L. Redleaf, The Family Defense Center, March 14, 2014
http://www.familydefensecenter.net/medical-ethics-concerns-in-child-abuse-investigations/

5. "BURDEN OF PROOF BEGONE: THE PERNICIOUS EFFECT OF EMERGENCY REMOVAL IN CHILD PROTECTIVE PROCEEDINGS," by Paul Chill, University of Connecticut School of Law, Family Court Review, October 2003
http://onlinelibrary.wiley.com/doi/10.1111/j.174-1617.2003.tb00907.x/abstract

6. "Parents Claim Nationwide Children's Hospital Violated Rights After Reporting Alleged Abuse," By Kevin Landers, WBNS-10TV, February 24, 2015

7. The Child Abuse Pediatrician (CAP) – Just Another Term for Medical "Cop," by Phil Locke, The Wrongful Convictions Blog, March 20, 2014
http://wrongfulconvictionsblog.org/2014/03/20/the-child-abuse-pediatrician-cap-just-another-term-for-medical-cop/

8. "Parents Wrongly Accused of Child Abuse Struggle to Get Kids Back," by Rachel Blustain, The Daily Beast, April 13, 2012
http://www.thedailybeast.com/articles/2012/04/13/parents-wrongly-accused-of-child-abuse-struggle-to-get-kids-back.html

9. "Hospital Video Surveillance," February 27, 2014
http://drwhitecoat.com/hospital-video-surveillance/

10. "Evaluation of covert video surveillance in the diagnosis of Munchausen syndrome by proxy: lessons from 41 cases," Journal of Pediatrics, June 2000
http://www.ncbi.nlm.nih.gov/pubmed/10835073

11. "Covert video surveillance: an important investigative tool or a breach of trust?" Archives of Disease in Childhood (peer-reviewed journal)
http://adc.bmj.com/content/81/4/291.full

12. "Covert video surveillance can be useful in abuse cases, but some reason for caution," Healthcare Risk Management, AHC Media, Feb. 2007
http://www.ahcmedia.com/articles/101003-covert-video-surveillance-can-be-useful-in-abuse-cases-but-some-reason-for-caution

Chaper 4: From Child Protection to State-sponsored Child Kidnapping: How Did we Get Here?

1. 10 Ancient Cultures That Practiced Ritual Human Sacrifice," by Paul Jongko, TopTenz.net, July 29, 2014
http://www.toptenz.net/10-ancient-cultures-practiced-ritual-human-sacrifice.php

2. Relics of Carthage Show Brutality Amid the Good Life," by Malcolm W. Browne, New York Times, published: September 1, 1987
http://www.nytimes.com/1987/09/01/science/relics-of-carthage-show-brutality-amid-the-good-life.html

3. "The History of Child Abuse," by Lloyd deMause, The Journal of Psychohistory 25 (3) Winter, 1998.
http://psychohistory.com/articles/the-history-of-child-abuse/

4. Lawson, J. Letter. New England Journal of Medicine, (May 26, 1988):P. 1198
http://www.nocirc.org/symposia/second/chamberlain.html

5. "The History of Child Abuse," by Lloyd deMause, The Journal of Psychohistory 25 (3) Winter 1998.

6. Social Work and Child Sexual Abuse (Journal of Social Work and Human Sexuality, Vol 1, No 1/2) , by David A. Shore and Jon Conte, published by Routledge (1982), p. 22

7. The Checkered Career of Parens Patriae: The State as Parent or Tyrant? By George B. Curtis, DePaul Law Review, Volume 25, Issue 4 Summer 1976.
http://via.library.depaul.edu/

8. "Civil Commitment: Past, Present, and Future," An Address by Paul F. Stavis at the National Conference of the National Alliance for the Mentally Ill, Washington, D.C. July 21, 1995.

http://www.treatmentadvocacycenter.org/component/content/article/360

9. www.americanbar.org "A Short History of Child Protection in America" By John E.B. Myers, *Family Law Quarterly*, Volume 42, Number 3, Fall 2008 pp. 450-455.

10. Thomas S. Szasz, *Law, Liberty and Psychiatry* (New York: Macmillan, 1963), p. 151.

11. PBS series, "Failure to Protect," FRONTLINE, January 2003.
http://www.pbs.org/wgbh/pages/frontline/shows/fostercare/inside/asfa.html

12. PBS series, "Failure to Protect," FRONTLINE, January 2003.
http://www.pbs.org/wgbh/pages/frontline/shows/fostercare/inside/roberts.html

13. Hession's blog, "Mass Outrage"
http://www.massoutrage.com/how–why-can-dcf-kidnap-your-child.html

14. "Parens Patriae: A Flawed Strategy for State-Initiated Obesity Litigation" John B. Hoke, 54 Wm. & Mary L. Rev. 1753 (2013),
http://scholarship.law.wm.edu/wmlr/vol54/iss5/7

15. "Parental Rights Amendment Inclusive of Parents with Disabilities," ParentalRights.org newsletter, October 27, 2015

16. "Parens Patriae: A Flawed Strategy for State-Initiated Obesity Litigation" John B. Hoke, 54 Wm. & Mary L. Rev. 1753 (2013),
http://scholarship.law.wm.edu/wmlr/vol54/iss5/7

Chapter 5: Does the State Ever Have a "Right" to Remove Children from a Home?

1. Cornell University Law School – Legal Information Institute – Due Process
https://www.law.cornell.edu/wex/due_process

2. *New Missouri Bill Filed to Prevent Medical Kidnapping*
http://medicalkidnap.com/2015/01/14/new-missouri-bill-filed-to-prevent-medical-kidnapping/

3. *"Justina's Law" Seeks to End Experimental Medical Research on Children Seized by Child Protection Services*
http://medicalkidnap.com/2014/06/28/justinas-law-seeks-to-end-experimental-medical-research-on-children-seized-by-child-protection-services/

4. *"Street Fighter" Attorney Takes On Riverside California CPS with Class Action Lawsuit*
http://medicalkidnap.com/2014/12/17/street-fighter-attorney-takes-on-riverside-california-cps-with-class-action-lawsuit/

5. *San Diego Police: "We're Not Changing Anything" – Seizure of Children to Continue*
http://medicalkidnap.com/2014/12/22/san-diego-police-were-not-changing-anything-seizure-of-children-to-continue/

6. *CPS Threatens to Take Children Away from Parents for Letting Them Walk to the Park*
http://medicalkidnap.com/2015/01/16/cps-threatens-to-take-children-away-from-parents-for-letting-them-walk-to-the-park/#sthash.mTr688yJ.dpuf

Chapter 6: A Tribute to Congresswoman Nancy Schaefer – Exposing State-sponsored Kidnappings

1. *What really took 2 lives in Schaefer case?* By Mark Davis – The Atlanta Journal-Constitution, April 4, 2010

2. *Nancy Shaefer, conservative activist, killed* – Baptist Press, March 29, 2010

3. *Update on the strange death of Nancy Schaefer* – News from Underground Blog – April 10, 2010